Islands in the Snow

A journey to explore
Nepal's trekking peaks

MARK HORRELL

Published by Mountain Footsteps Press

Copyright © 2018 Mark Horrell
www.markhorrell.com
All rights reserved

First published as an ebook 2011
Revised edition published 2018

Except where indicated all photographs
copyright © Mark Horrell

ISBN (paperback): 978-1-912748-02-0
ISBN (ebook): 978-1-912748-01-3

"I now had about six weeks to roam, explore, and climb as the spirit might move me. But first I visited the leader and others at Camp I. I went up there in a holiday mood, persuading myself of the advantages of for once being at the foot of a high mountain without any obligation of having to try and climb it."

Col. Jim Roberts

ISLANDS
IN THE
SNOW

Footsteps on the Mountain
Travel Diaries

DAY 1
THE WORLD'S SCARIEST AIRPORT

Wednesday, 22 April 2009 – Phuiyan, Solu-Khumbu, Nepal

It's the third time in my life that I've experienced the hair-raising flight from Kathmandu to Lukla. We are only just starting our trip, and already we've suffered a setback. Yesterday we spent eight hours sitting in Kathmandu Airport waiting for the Lukla flight to be declared good to go.

It feels like these flights tread a line between marginally safe and completely insane. As you descend, the airstrip in Lukla emerges out of the clouds, perched on a ledge ahead of you. But a fatal accident occurred last October. Clouds swept in front of the pilot's line of sight just as he was about to land. He missed the runway and caught the plane's wing in a fence to the left of the narrow landing strip. The plane caught fire, and eighteen passengers and crew were killed. The authorities are now more cautious about letting flights land in overcast conditions.

I'm here in Nepal with my friend and climbing

partner Mark Dickson for a month of trekking and climbing. We're hoping to complete a circuit of the Solu-Khumbu region, climbing the popular trekking peaks of Mera Peak (6,476m) and Island Peak (6,189m) on the way. It's our warm up for a much bigger expedition to Pakistan later in the year.

I've been looking forward to this trek for a few years now, ever since climbing Mera Peak for the first time five years ago. I have never climbed Island Peak (though Mark has), but many people have told me about the trail connecting the two peaks, which crosses a high, technical pass called the Amphu Labtsa. The pass is so high that it's permanently glaciated and is considered to be as challenging as the two summits. The combination of beautiful, remote trekking and accessible peaks is the thing that most attracts me to Nepal, and my heart flutters with excitement at the start of every trip.

This time my excitement has been delayed.

We checked in for our flight at 6.30am yesterday. At 2.30pm, Yeti Airlines were the last operator to abandon the wait. We trudged back to the Hotel Shanker, where Mark was dismayed to learn we were back in Room 117 – the same room we'd checked out of earlier in the morning.

He looked downcast.

'They could at least have put us in a different room. This just underlines the fact that we haven't gone anywhere today.'

But Mark has his own way of seeking consolation. A few minutes later we found ourselves downstairs in the unfortunately named Kunti Bar, discussing contingencies with Siling, our friend and trekking guide who organised the logistics for our expedition. A few hours later, we were the last people to leave Sam's Bar in Thamel for the third evening in a row.

To avoid any unnecessary waiting this morning, Siling decides to go to the airport on his own and give us a call if the flights start leaving. Mark and I have a comparative lie-in before Siling gives us the good news and we jump in a taxi to catch a 10.30 flight.

Mountain flights in Nepal feel so unreal they're almost like being in a dream. This is the third time I've taken the Lukla flight, and I'm still not getting used to it. Wedged in a sixteen-seat Twin Otter plane with my rucksack on my lap, I can see the cockpit door wide open in front of me.

One of the pilots is reading a newspaper. This isn't at all comforting, so I decide to look through the window to my left.

I see giant ridges of rock and snow spilling out of the clouds on the horizon high above. I try to name the peaks, but they are unrecognisable at this height. First there is a twin-peaked summit that Siling tells me is Gauri Sankar, then a horribly precipitous corniced ridge of ice that I can't identify. I make out a broad dome of snow that I believe must be Cho Oyu, the sixth-highest mountain in the world, then another massive peak – probably Gyachung Kang – then a convoluted maze of snow that can only be the Pumori-Everest-Lhotse-Nuptse massif.

These peaks look so different from the air it's hard

to work out the lie of the ridgelines and be sure which is which. The closest one, which looks the highest, is probably Lhotse, the fourth-highest mountain in the world, with Everest, the highest, just behind. I imagine that I can make out a smaller ridge beneath its towering south face that might just be Island Peak – one of our objectives for this expedition. I'm probably wrong, though. The only mountain I feel confident of identifying is Chamlang, a sheer and distinctive half disc to the east of the main range, which I saw at a similar angle from high camp on Mera Peak five years ago.

Then I feel the plane begin to descend, and I turn my attention to the terrain not so far beneath me. Thick forests climb up steep mountain slopes. The peaks are cut apart by gorges that foam with water. It takes a leap of faith to believe there's anywhere around here flat enough to support an airstrip. But then we bank right and the valley widens a little as we make towards a cluster of houses on a precipitous hillside high above a river. We are now flying directly towards the side of a hill that rises many thousands of metres above the plane. If I didn't know any better I'd think we were about to crash straight into it, but then I feel the wheels touch down with a jolt and we brake up a very steep runway. It's a safe landing.

We've landed head-on to a narrow ledge high above the gorge. The airstrip at Lukla is built on a steep gradient so that planes can brake more quickly to prevent crashing into the mountain wall beyond. It's a strategy that usually works, but it's not one for people with a fear of flying.

We have Sir Edmund Hillary to thank for this experience. After making the first ascent of Everest with Tenzing Norgay in 1953, the legendary New Zealander extended his gratitude to the Sherpa people by setting up a charity, the Himalayan Trust, which helped to build schools and hospitals in the Khumbu region. In those days, building supplies still needed to be carried in by porters on foot, so in 1964 Hillary started looking for a suitable site for a runway – not easy in that mountainous region. He was approached by a group of farmers from Lukla, offering a large area of rough pasture, heavy scrub and potato fields. It wasn't completely flat, but he realised it could be used by short take-off and landing (STOL) aircraft. It so happened that Twin Otter planes were being developed, and the first one flew in 1965. Hillary bought the land on behalf of the Nepalese government for US$635, and the airport now carries his name, as well as that of Tenzing.

We spill out onto the runway and walk across the tarmac to a gate beside the terminal building. Within five minutes, our gear has been unloaded and replaced with return cargo, and other passengers have boarded the Twin Otter. The plane accelerates down the runway then drops like a stone out of sight into the gorge. A few seconds later, it reappears and rises again on its way back to Kathmandu.

It seems we've been lucky today. The flights from Kathmandu usually arrive in Lukla only minutes apart, but as we wander through the blue-roofed stone houses of Lukla village – most of them tourist lodges – there are no more planes coming in. We notice that the wind has picked up. It looks like we managed to catch the very last one before flights were suspended again.

Looking towards Lukla airstrip from the balcony of the North Face Lodge

Mark and I spend the next two hours relaxing in the North Face Lodge while Siling and his staff load up our supplies for the expedition. No fewer than eight porters and four kitchen staff will be supporting us, as well as Siling and our climbing guide Dawa. As they get organised, we chat idly to the many trekkers returning from their Everest Base Camp treks en route to catching flights back to Kathmandu. They are surprised and envious when we tell them our plans.

We're out here for five weeks; then in June, we intend to go to Pakistan and spend two months attempting a much bigger mountain called Gasherbrum.

'However do you manage to get the time off work?' someone says.

This is a question I am often asked, and it has a straightforward answer.

'I gave up my job,' I reply. 'I do contract work. I'll get another one when I go back.'

'Me too,' Mark says.

We set off walking at 1.30. The trail immediately drops 500m into the valley as it snakes around a hillside high above the river. After crossing a steep side stream at a small village, we're faced with a long hot climb to regain the height we've lost. We stop to rest from time to time, and the porters usually stop with us. They all seem in high spirits.

'Have they been drinking?' I ask Siling.

He laughs. 'No, they're all friends from the same village.'

Although it's early days, he seems happy with them. As our sirdar, he's in overall charge of logistics for the expedition, and keeping large numbers of porters working together for a month can often be a problem. The fact these porters know each other already is going to help.

The sun beats fiercely as we trek in and out of villages. From time to time the trail flattens out or passes into the shade of the oaks and pines that cling densely to the valley sides. These moments are brief, but they provide welcome relief from the heat. We are on the regular trail to the roadhead at Jiri, six days' walk away. While most trekkers fly in to Lukla and skip the extra six days of trekking from Jiri, most supplies are brought in by foot rather than air, and we meet plenty of porters carrying laden baskets to replenish the many tourist lodges further up.

After walking for two hours, we stop for tea at a lodge near the top of a steep climb. It has a pleasant garden terrace lined with flower tubs, looking back up the valley to Lukla. As we sit and sip our tea, we hear the faint buzz of an engine getting louder. We watch three planes pass by in quick succession and disappear into the hillside at Lukla. They are the only planes to land since we arrived at 11.15. I still find it difficult to believe there's an airstrip in that precipitous landscape.

We arrive at Phuiyan at five o'clock – another of the many villages clinging to the hillside well above the Dudh Kosi River. We stop at a lodge with a flat grassy garden overlooking the valley, where we can pitch our tents for the night. We're entertained by half a dozen kids playing with a stick. Siling explains the rules of a game called *Dundibu*, which he describes as the national sport of Nepal. One team digs a small trench and lays a stick across it. They take it in turns to flick the stick over the heads of the opposition using a second stick. The opposition then try to throw the first stick into the trench from where it lands. The third part of the game is even more eccentric. It involves laying the first stick on the ground and bashing it with the second one. This causes the first stick to fly into the air, and while it's airborne, they whack it as far as possible with the second stick. If it sounds complicated, that's because it is.

I study the kids as they dart to and fro, sticks held aloft. 'It sounds a bit silly to me. Do the sticks have names?'

Mark roars with laughter. 'What, you mean like Mingma and Pasang?'

'Not those kind of names, you idiot. Like in snooker you have a cue ball and an object ball. Maybe you have a flick stick and a whacking stick.'

'A whacking stick. What the hell do you do with a whacking stick?'

Siling helps me out by explaining the rules of a second game, which he describes as the national sport of India.

'Hang on, isn't cricket the national sport of India?'

Now Siling laughs. 'Cricket? And you tell me Dundibu is silly.'

I shut up.

After dinner in the lodge, we meet the rest of our staff. We've already met our climbing leader Dawa, who waited with us at the airport yesterday and walked with us today. Mark and I know all but one of our kitchen staff – Sarki the cook, and his three assistants Gombu, Pasang and Karma – from an expedition to Chulu Far East last autumn. I try to memorise the names of our eight porters Lhakpa, Temba, Pema, Wongchu, Bujung, Drukchen, Tashi and Pemba – but it's going to be difficult.

When it's our turn to introduce ourselves, I realise

it's going to be much easier for them.

'I'm Mark,' I tell them.

'And I'm also Mark,' Mark says.

DAY 2
DEHYDRATION

Thursday, 23 April 2009 – Pangkongma, Solu-Khumbu, Nepal

Today is not one of my better days. I wake up inside the tent in the middle of the night. I'm feeling nauseous, and by morning I'm worse. I diagnose my illness fairly quickly – it's dehydration, and it's self-inflicted. I blame Mark for some of my misery. He made me spend three days boozing in Kathmandu. But it's my fault that I walked at a crazy rate yesterday, racing up and down hillsides in hot sun without replenishing enough fluid. I should know better by now. Lukla is at 2,800m, sufficiently low that I assumed I would have no trouble acclimatising. Had I taken things sensibly then this would be true. But good acclimatisation is all about keeping hydrated and taking it easy, two principles I forgot, and now I'm suffering for it.

I end up feeling nauseous all day. I'm unable to eat at breakfast or at lunch, and no matter how much I drink, I can't seem to pee. My lethargy leads to a slow pace as I struggle along, sweating in the hot sun.

It's such a waste. It would be a pleasant day's walking if only I could appreciate it. For the first hour of the morning we continue to contour around on the main Jiri trail, spending much of our time in gloomy rhododendron forest before the sun has had a chance to rise from behind the mountains. Then we leave the main trail on a steep path and climb a shoulder leading into a side valley. At the top of the shoulder stands a lonely peasant hut that on a clear day would command views right up the Dudh Kosi Valley to Cho Oyu. The sun shines and the setting is tranquil, but the 8,000m giant remains hidden behind a wispy cloud.

I walk with Mark, Siling and Dawa for some of the day, but Mark is much quicker than me. He has already been on a warm-up trek in the Langtang region of Nepal, but more importantly, he's not ill. He and Dawa disappear off ahead while Siling slows down to keep me company.

We see tonight's destination beyond the shoulder: the village of Pangkongma is perched across the valley opposite, a short distance beneath the Pangkongma La pass. As we look between colourful pinks and reds of rhododendron trees, it seems a daunting prospect in my pitiful state, and the hours pass slowly. We descend 600m on a rocky path that winds around the head of the valley, then climb back up to Pangkongma at an altitude of 2,850m. It should have been an easy day, but I crawl into the village exhausted.

I fall asleep in the dining room of a teahouse eclectically plastered with colourful posters of mountains, Buddhist monks, scantily clad Bollywood actresses, and a frightening photo of a giant baby against a purple background.

Luckily my condition improves as the evening progresses – no thanks to Siling trying to keep my spirits up with his jokes. He tells us one shaggy-dog story about a porter called Pemba who carries loads between Lukla and Namche. Every evening Pemba wakes his landlady when he comes home drunk and throws his boots across the room. The story goes on for about five minutes, but it seems like more. The ending is terrible. The landlady complains; the next night Pemba throws one boot off, but remembers to take the second off quietly.

'And then the landlady stays awake for the rest of the night waiting for the second boot to clatter across the room,' Siling says.

There is a pause as we wait for the punchline. It doesn't come; instead, Siling just giggles.

'Is that it?' says Mark. 'Dear me. If all your jokes are as bad as that, I'm going to look forward to hearing some of Mark's.'

DAY 3
INTO THE HINKU VALLEY

Friday, 24 April 2009 – Nashing Dingma, Solu-Khumbu, Nepal

I wake in much better shape this morning. As if in sympathy for my recent toils, the sky is completely clear with not a cloud in sight, and it remains so for most of the day. This is just as well, as it's a longer walk today, with more ascent and descent in hot sun.

We begin by plodding slowly up to the Pangkongma La, the first high pass of our trek, 250m above the village. I stop occasionally to look back. The twin mountains of Dudh Kunde and Karyolang rise across the valley, one a white ridge and the other a rocky triangle. Less obvious is an attractive monastery perched neatly in forest above the village.

Luckily for Siling, he's only taken half a dozen photos when he notices there's no film in his camera.

'You still have a film camera – why don't you get with the times and go digital?' I say.

He giggles nervously.

Beyond the pass we find ourselves 1,000m above

the Hinku Valley, which stretches wide and deep before us. We have an immediate descent to the valley floor only to climb back up the other side. But this is Nepal – such paths are inevitable and quickly forgotten against a backdrop of soaring mountains. Shortly after crossing the pass we see Mera Peak for the first time, its three webbed summits rising above a line of ridges further up the valley. All being well, we plan to climb each of them in about a week's time.

An early view of the three summits of Mera Peak: Mera North, Mera Central and the trekking summit

Colourful rhododendrons in flowering reds and pinks carpet the hillsides around us. They're so pretty that at one point I even see Mark stooping to photograph a radiant bloom.

'Photographing flowers again, Mark?' I say as I

pass.

'Fuck off.'

It seems to take next to no time to complete our descent through charred woodland to the valley floor. As early as eleven o'clock we stop for lunch at a teahouse about 50m above the bridge. The teahouse hadn't been built when I came this way in 2004, and it's as mellow a spot for lunch as you can find anywhere. A grassy promontory extends from a hillside above the river, which crashes past 100m below us, and a canopied table and benches provide some shade from the hot sun. The gorge is narrow here. A little upstream we can gaze down on a series of turquoise rock pools joined together by milk-white cascades.

Mark shows us an amazing photo of two colourful roller birds perching on a branch, which he took on safari in Bardia National Park a couple of weeks ago. He's managed to capture the moment when one of them is launching into flight.

'I dreamed about that,' Siling says.

'What, of a roller bird launching into flight?' I ask.

'No, about Mark showing me the photo of it.'

I look across the table, expecting Mark to launch into some sarcastic comment about Siling's mystical powers.

I'm surprised when he replies: 'Yeah, that sometimes happens to me.'

I have to play Mark's part for him.

'Oh, I see. I didn't know you could do that, Milarepa,' I say, likening Siling to the 11th-century

Buddhist poet and master who spent his life in the Tibetan borderland area where Siling grew up.

Siling laughs, but I'm not sure Mark knows who Milarepa is.

Just below our lunch spot, a footbridge crosses the Hinku Khola, suspended between two rocks. It hangs a full 50m above the crashing river, but luckily it's of sturdy steel construction. These Himalayan suspension bridges are not for those of a nervous disposition. I don't have the best head for heights, but I manage to remain calm by concentrating on the strands of metal beneath my feet as the bridge sways to my tread.

The afternoon's walk consists of a single long climb, first through steep pastureland (*kharka*) cut into terraces, then rhododendron forest. At one point, we stop for water beside a woven grass shack where we saw some of our porters stop a few minutes earlier. We hear raucous laughter broken by the occasional giggles of a female voice. Siling pokes his head around the door to see what's going on, and comes back out with a bemused look on his face.

'These boys are so gregarious. Whenever they find a girl, they tease and tease and tease her.'

'Yeah, I've noticed we always seem to stop in teahouses where there's a girl,' Mark says.

'She is on her own because her husband has gone trekking,' Siling says. He pauses thoughtfully, before adding: 'I hope he isn't teasing women too.'

We arrive at Nashing Dingma (2,630m) at 3.15. The village sits on a wide grassy platform on the even wider expanse of the Hinku Valley's upper reaches. Unusually for this part of Nepal, this means the sun remains overhead until about six o'clock, when it finally disappears behind a mountain. This is prime pasture – I expect I will have to get used to the sound of cows mooing outside my tent.

The porters disperse to stay the night in the half dozen shacks dotted around the village. We watch them go, and I wonder how they choose their accommodation.

'That's not hard to guess,' Mark replies. 'Hmm... I wonder which houses have girls living in them.'

He goes on to expound his theory of natural selection in the Himalayas, which involves the slowest porters arriving late, and having to bed down in a stable owned by the most decrepit man in the village.

'It's an interesting theory, Mark,' I reply. 'But I don't think Charles Darwin will need to relinquish his crown just yet.'

DAY 4
BAMBOO FOREST

Saturday, 25 April 2009 – Chalen Kharka, Solu-Khumbu, Nepal

We leave Nashing Dingma, in green pasture land, at 7.45, and immediately climb 300m through forest to another pass, the Surke La. We meet a Polish trekker on his way to Tumlingtar in eastern Nepal. He can't believe it when I pay 150 rupees (about US$1.50) for a Snickers bar in a tea shop at the pass. He offers me his fare of doughnuts and samosas, which he says cost him 10 rupees each. He's been living off them for a month while he treks around the Khumbu. I ask him whether he's ever been ill.

'When I first arrived I had diarrhoea for several days, but then I got used to the food and I'm fine now,' he replies.

Having saved up a few quid for this trip, I'd rather do without the diarrhoea – I decline his offer. My self-inflicted twenty-four hours of dehydration were enough for me.

He and his Israeli companion have been trekking

around the Khumbu on their own with no support, no tents and no cooking equipment. They've been staying with locals and buying food from them. At the risk of stereotyping, these are two nationalities with a reputation for miserly travelling habits, and I suspect they may find our fully supported expedition with porters, kitchen staff and climbing guides difficult to comprehend. The high glacier regions through which we'll be travelling preclude any possibility of staying with locals or finding food along the way, but even if they didn't, I'd certainly pay for the luxury of a tent and the opportunity for someone else to carry the load off my back if I can afford it. I am here on holiday, and want to enjoy the moment, not just look back on it with fond memories.

Many people see shoestring independent travel as a purer form of adventure. Although I can understand this point of view, it's not the only valid one. It may be just the thing when you're hard up, but there are other benefits to our way of doing things. Seeing the way our porters – who are all friends from the same village – seem to be enjoying themselves, I'm sure they're glad of the employment, and the chance to take pleasure in the camaraderie of being out on trek as part of a team.

Steep steps above the Surke La lead up to a viewpoint, and I climb them with Mark, Siling and Dawa. The view is hazy with all the dust and smoke from forest fires that blaze at this time of year. We're not yet deep enough into the Khumbu to see any of the giant snow peaks, but the forested hills around and beneath us are awash with colour: many shades of green, the pinks and reds of rhododendrons, and the occasional white of a flowering magnolia.

We take lunch in a patch of boggy grassland a little down from the pass but on the same broad ridge. Here Mark falls asleep and I read my book. After lunch we climb through forest. Last time I came this way I remember ascending through bamboo forest in a veil of grey mist with nothing to see beyond about 100m. Today, despite the haze, it's much more pleasant, and we take it at an easy pace – so slowly that Sarki and Dawa have time to stop and cut long sticks of bamboo from the trees. When they get to camp they intend to trim them down into straws for drinking *tongba*, a local alcoholic drink. We stop to wait for them on a pleasant grassy promontory overlooking pasture land on the hills far beneath the forest.

'Would you do that, Mark – drink your beer through a straw?' I ask.

'I have done,' he replies. 'It gets you pissed more quickly.'

He used to be a rugby player.

We continue through mixed forest of bamboo, rhododendron and juniper. A short while later we arrive at Chalen Kharka (3,580m), our campsite on a wide ridge, where terraced platforms have been cut for tents. Although forest ascends the ridges either side of us, the campsite is located in an area where taller trees give way to low-standing shrubs, so there is nothing around us to obscure the view. The first major pass of the trek, the Chalen La, towers high above us in rocky terrain between two summits well above the tree line. Tomorrow we pass between this gateway up to higher altitudes.

Ascending through forest to Chalen Kharka

DAY 5
INTO HIGH MOORLAND

Sunday, 26 April 2009 – Chanbu Kharka, Solu-Khumbu, Nepal

We start this morning with an ascent of over 600m to the Chalen La, a high pass at 4,250m. We could see it from camp, nestling between a prominent rock gateway.

Again I take it *bistari, bistari* (slowly, slowly) as I watch Mark and Dawa disappear up the slope above us. Not far out of our campsite, the path climbs above the juniper into open, shrubby grassland. About halfway up, Siling and I come over a brow where Mark and Dawa are waiting by an abandoned stone hut. The view here opens out across the Hinku Valley – which we have been climbing away from – and towards Karyolang, a mountain that has been appearing on and off since we began the trek. We watch a bright blue grandala and its white-winged mate hop across the stones of the building.

Since I last came this way in 2004, someone has been busy cutting steps. We climb the remainder of the distance to the gateway on a 350m stone staircase, stopping frequently to watch alpine accentors and robin accentors skittering about on the rocks either side. Mark is waiting for us at the gateway; Dawa has ascended a little further up to the summit that formed the right-hand gatepost as we looked from camp.

Mark Dickson, Dawa and Siling take a rest
during the ascent to the Chalen La

Last night in the mess tent he was reading the somewhat heavy *Interim Constitution for the Government of Nepal.*

'I think you'll find he's genuinely interested in politics,' Mark says. 'On the way up, we've been discussing the new constitution, wind turbines, freedom of religion, and land rights of indigenous groups.'

'His English must be better than I thought if you've managed to get through all that,' I reply.

But while Dawa may have revealed a deeper side, the same cannot be said of our merry band of porters. We traverse for a while beyond the gateway and then start climbing again to another pass. Four of the porters overtake me and start laughing.

'If I were carrying a load like they are, I wouldn't want to speak to anyone, let alone have a laugh with them,' I say to Siling. 'What were they laughing at this time?'

'One of them just farted,' he replies.

The pass eventually rises to 4,425m before descending past the sacred Panch Pokhari lakes, where tridents to the Hindu god Shiva have been left by the shore. It was rather more atmospheric last time I came this way. As we descended through thick mist and spied the tridents thrusting from the lakeside through the gloom, I kept expecting to see a hand emerge from the water clasping the sword *Excalibur*.

There is no such drama this time. Although it's starting to cloud over a little, the view is extensive, first to the dark blue lakes below us, and then beyond to the campsite at Chanbu Kharka.

Chanbu Kharka sits in a natural hanging amphitheatre enclosed by rock walls on three sides. A river runs through the bowl and plunges down waterfalls on the open side into the Hinku Valley a couple of thousand metres below. We were expecting to see a pink-clad, ponytailed French-Canadian trekker here – he camped with us at Chalen Kharka and set off before us this morning – but we have the place to ourselves. Siling explains that he's continued to the next campsite a few hours further on and several hundred metres lower.

At Chalen Kharka, the French-Canadian trekker came over and asked us if we were sticking to the *3-500m rule*. We looked at him blankly before we realised he wasn't a very experienced trekker. Someone must have told him that you could only ascend 300 to 500m a day if you wanted to avoid altitude sickness. Mark gave him some helpful advice about acclimatisation, such as taking Diamox if he's worried, or camping a little higher and spending a night there before descending again.

'Six hundred metres is no problem,' Mark reassured him.

But now it appears that the man has ignored this advice.

'Oh, I know why he's not camping here,' Mark says. A look in his eye suggests that a light bulb has flashed on inside his head. 'He's sticking to the *3-500m rule*. Didn't I tell you he was an idiot. What's he going to do when he climbs Mera Peak – camp every three hundred metres?'

It looks like the French-Canadian has decided to compress two days of walking into one in order to avoid camping high like we are. This is actually more likely to result in altitude sickness – instead of taking it easy today, he has had a long day and will have risked overexerting.

Now that we've seen a few bird and tree species

over the last few days, I bring my wildlife book of eastern Nepal to afternoon tea, to help us identify some of the things we've seen so far. Siling browses through it and comes across the entry for alder. He seems to have a mine of old Nepali folk tales, and this prompts him to recount one of them.

Back home in the UK, alder is often the first tree species to take root along river banks, before the larger species such as willow and birch. In Nepal, the alder is usually the first species to take root in the dry earth left behind by a landslide.

'There is a reason for this,' Siling tells us. 'When he was a young boy, Alder was one of the most handsome and eligible boys in the forest. When it was time for Alder to take a wife, the local priest said that such a handsome boy ought to wed the most beautiful girl in all the land.

'So he took him high into the hills to meet Rhododendron and her family, for them to be introduced and betrothed if they were seen to be compatible. But they went in the middle of winter, and when they entered the room Alder said to the priest, "I can't see Rhododendron – which one is she?" The priest pointed out a small girl curled up in the corner, not at all resembling the colourful girl he had been led to expect. "Oh, I can't marry her," Alder said. "Come on, let's go."

'Time went on, and many years later Alder had still not found a wife. One day his work took him back into the hills again. It was May and everyone around him seemed to be blooming. Then he spied the most beautiful girl he could imagine, clad all in pink, and he realised with a shudder that it was the same Rhododendron he'd been introduced to all those years ago. Unable to bear the consequences of the mistake he'd made, he decided to kill himself by throwing himself off the nearest cliff. And that is why the alder is always the first to take root after a landslide.'

'Hmm. That's not the most cheerful folk story I've ever heard,' Mark says. 'But at least it's better than some of your jokes.'

DAY 6
MIRKWOOD

Monday, 27 April 2009 – Kote, Solu-Khumbu, Nepal

The sky above the basin was cloudless by the time we turned in last night, but I thought I could discern a grey, ghostly mist rising up from the Hinku Valley on the open side. Whether this portends anything sinister for today, I don't know; when I wake up this morning it's clear and sunny, though still very cold.

While we wait for the porters to finish packing all our gear and move away, I take my binoculars up a hillside and watch the grandalas, white-capped redstarts and accentors hopping around between the rocks. I even spy a neatly camouflaged grey pika – a tiny rock-hopping rabbit-like creature – munching on grass before disappearing into its burrow beneath a boulder.

The day's trek starts with a short climb out of the amphitheatre. At the top, I pause and look back across at the Panch Pokhari lakes at a similar height on the opposite side of the Chanbu Kharka bowl. Beyond, a black jagged line marks the ridge we traversed from the Chalen La to Panch Pokhari. The way forward from here is an unlikely path hundreds of metres above the Hinku Khola. The river is so far beneath us we can't even see it, let alone hear it. Again Mark and Dawa walk far ahead of us. Siling and I traverse the path, skipping from boulder to boulder as it weaves around the hillside. Thin cloud touches the hilltops around us. We're well above the tree line now, though plenty of grass merges into the rocks.

After a while we catch up with Mark and Dawa waiting for us on a grassy headland where the path begins its descent to the river. Mark sits perched at the top of a rock buttress thrusting dramatically out of the valley. I take a seat beside him and rest for twenty minutes, basking in the tranquil scene. I look out over the valley and survey the white tops of Kusum Kangguru and Kyashar appearing in and out of cloud on the opposite side.

Then we begin the long descent to the valley floor, first angling down the hillside across rocky terrain, then touching the fringes of rhododendron forest as the path continues to traverse the hillside. Finally, we plunge into a steep descent through the forest.

Towards the bottom of the slope we find ourselves in fantastically primeval woodland. Huge fir trees laden with sheets of lichen spill their ancient roots over giant boulders. The path is laddered with roots and mossy carpets, and every few metres shafts of vertical sunlight spill through the canopy to light the trail. Clumps of purple primulas cluster beside the path near these sunnier patches, and smaller rhododendrons – some with leaves the size of dinner plates – cower beneath the fir trees. The whole setting is like something out of *The Lord of the Rings*. When I sit down to rest on a low-hanging branch, I expect to discover I'm sitting on Treebeard's hand. It would not have surprised me had I been lifted a few metres off the ground to find myself gazing into the eyes of a giant walking tree (well, perhaps I would have been a little surprised).

Karma, the youngest of the kitchen assistants, suddenly appears on the path in front of us carrying a kettle of hot lemon and four cups. Sarki has given up waiting for us at our lunch stop and sent him along the trail to meet us. We stop and drink before moving on, and a few minutes later we emerge from the forest into the valley floor. In its upper reaches the Hinku Valley is one long boulder field through which the river powers a route. The sides of the valley are so steep that a grey gravel apron 5m high lines its base on both sides, where regular landslides have smashed the trees away. Above the gravel apron, forests climb steep hillsides.

We have lunch on a blue tarpaulin laid out between rocks, then dive back into the fringes of the forest to complete the walk up the valley to the village of Kote. Here wooden shacks perch above the noisy river; most have terraced gardens for trekkers' camping grounds. We stop at one and pitch our tents for the night.

When I came here in 2004, Kote was a stronghold

for the Maoists, who had been waging an insurgency against the government since 1996. While they had terrorised the local population in many rural parts of Nepal, they generally left tourists alone. I was affected briefly on my first visit to Nepal in 2002, when the Maoists called a general strike and we had to travel by road a day earlier than planned. Drivers lived in fear of their lives if they broke a strike by working, but tourists trapped in urban areas found themselves inconvenienced at worst. The main effect for trekkers was a *tourist tax* we had to pay if we hiked through Maoist-controlled areas. This happened to me when I trekked the Annapurna Circuit in 2006. We passed a Maoist checkpoint where a well-spoken rebel politely asked us to hand over a hundred rupees per day for our trek, and presented us with a receipt to show to any other guerrillas who might stop us along the way.

Kote had been my first overt encounter with Maoists. People were strutting around with Kalashnikovs, and the buildings were scrawled with Maoist slogans. Our sirdar Kaji, a cool and calm person, had looked decidedly harassed. They told him he was carrying a dodgy receipt and needed to pay another 3,000 rupees for each member of the group. Our poor Sherpas felt intimidated, but as Kaji negotiated a compromise, we were left free from harassment in the dining room of a teahouse.

The bloody civil war, which by 2005 had killed more than 19,000 people, ended with the signing of a peace agreement in November 2006. The Maoists ceased their armed struggle and became a political party. Kote is now a different place – an ordinary Nepalese village with teahouses, just like any other.

During afternoon tea I spread my maps out and discuss the route ahead with Mark, Siling and Dawa. When I first climbed Mera Peak in 2004, a member of our group had T-shirts made back in Kathmandu, which displayed the altitude as 6,476m. But I was dismayed to look at my map and see that Mera Central, the peak we climbed, was only marked as 6,461m. It was actually one of Mera's other summits, Mera North, that was marked as 6,476m. Had we climbed the wrong peak?

I discovered later that, almost without exception, every trekking operator took their clients up Mera Central, yet none of them questioned whether Mera North might actually be higher. Most of them didn't even mention Mera North. In their turn, clients who are proud of their achievement at reaching the top, aren't willing to question whether the summit they reached was the true one.

Why do the operators do this? Is Mera Central higher, after all? There was only one way to find out: to climb both peaks and measure their altitudes with a GPS. I put this proposal to my teammates. Mark and Siling are both keen on the idea, but Dawa is our climbing guide, so he is the one whose opinion matters.

I point at the map and ask him what he thinks.

'Can we climb Mera North?'

'Yes, it is possible,' he says. 'We can try.'

When I return to my tent I can see that the clouds

have cleared up the valley, revealing Mera's dramatic south face sweeping nearly 3,000m above us. It rises beyond the forests of a side valley in a trio of summits like a flattened letter 'W'. The white line of a snowy cornice crowns all three tops. I know from my previous visit that this is the top end of gentle slopes which flow down the opposite side. Ascents from that side are far simpler, making the peak accessible to ordinary folk like me. From here the mountain looks altogether more daunting. I'm looking at the upper reaches of the South-West Pillar, a steep buttress of black rock and ice leading all the way up to the central summit.

When Mal Duff and Ian Tattersall made the first ascent of the pillar in 1986, they had as much trouble ascending a glacier to the foot of the mountain as they had climbing the face. A tumble of ice blocks gave way beneath Tattersall's feet as he climbed in and out of a crevasse. The ice disappeared into the bowels of the glacier, hundreds of metres below. Tattersall was able to keep his footing, but for a few brief seconds Duff thought he had disappeared into the crevasse. Later they reached a cul-de-sac in the glacier, and had no alternative but to crawl through a tunnel of ice forty-five metres long, sunlight barely visible at the far end. As they camped at the foot of the pillar, they watched seracs collapsing on the glacier they had just crossed.

The climb itself was no picnic; it involved 1,800m of ascent and two overnight bivouacs. The first day of ice climbing was straightforward, with good quality ice and secure belays on every pitch. The second day was much harder, much of it on badly rotten rock they decided to climb to avoid an overhang of steep ice and creaking granite. As they secured themselves on a ledge for their second bivouac, they noticed a swirling bank of clouds approaching, and they realised the following day was going to be pretty unpleasant.

They climbed with urgency up a 70° face of glassy ice which was so hard that Tattersall snapped the head off an ice screw trying to twist it into place. The storm arrived as they climbed the final rock pitches above the ice wall. A barrage of hailstones was flung across them, masking their holds and making it hard for them to find a route.

'We climbed to survive,' Duff later said, 'individual moves no longer fun, just a necessity.'

There was one more buttress of ice, which Duff led with a few dicey moves, then a rock ledge took them onto the summit.

'Only effort was required as we cruised down the standard route into the twilight,' Duff said about the descent.

This story reminds me why I'm a trekker, not a climber. It doesn't sound like fun to me, although I'm sure they experienced a great sense of achievement at the end of it. I prefer to 'cruise' up the easy route, though my previous ascent could more accurately be described as lurching than cruising.

DAY 7
A TINY GOMPA

Tuesday, 28 April 2009 – Tangnag, Makalu-Barun
National Park, Nepal

Kote marks the start of the Makalu-Barun National Park boundary. First thing this morning we have to stop at the national park checkpoint to have our permits stamped. Nepali kids besiege me as I wait, desperate to have their photos taken.

For most of the morning the path weaves in and out of boulders on the valley floor. After an hour or two it climbs a steep bank into yak pasture embedded with mossy rocks. Dwarf juniper and dwarf rhododendron carpet the ground and it's all very pleasant. We are now back on the main tourist trail. Several trekkers on their way back down from Mera Peak greet us; we're pleased to hear about their reasonable success rate in reaching the summit. The heavy snow from a couple of weeks ago – which we'd heard about in Kathmandu – appears to have gone, leaving the summit route clear again.

By 11.30 we arrive at a sheltered spot at the far end of the yak pasture. Here Sarki and the crew have laid out the blue tarpaulin for lunch, and we lie in the sun for a couple of hours. It's surprisingly warm given that we're now at 4,000m. Sarki's cuisine seems to have veered westwards – and I'm finding it much more palatable. Last night he cooked us pizza and chips. For lunch today I tuck in to fried potato, cauliflower in cheese, sausages and chapati before falling asleep among juniper thickets.

In the afternoon we stop at a lonely gompa (small monastery) hewn into a giant rock above the trail. This is reputedly one of the holiest gompas in the region. Siling had been hoping to ask the lama (monk) who lives here to conduct a puja – or blessing ceremony – for our successful ascent. The lama's not at home. We leave 50-rupee notes next to his gong to conduct the puja for us when he returns.

'It's funny, the bigger the mountain, the more seriously the puja is taken,' says Mark, who was on Everest last year. 'On Everest you have to carry out the ceremony on an auspicious day. Here you just leave some money and move on.'

A little further along the trail we stop for a rest outside another teahouse. Mark and I are waiting outside when Siling brings out a venerable old man wearing a red down jacket. He's smiling, keen to greet us, and I wonder who he is. Siling explains he's the lama from the gompa; only then do I notice he's wearing a red robe beneath his down jacket.

The lama invites us inside and offers us tea. He

possesses the cheerful, laughing countenance Buddhist monks from the Dalai Lama downwards all seem to possess. We have no common language, but he keeps smiling and pointing at his cheeks, asking me the word in English.

'Cheeks,' I say, but he shakes his head.

It takes a while to figure it out, but I eventually realise that he only laughs at me and points at his cheeks when I laugh at him. He has noticed that a strange thing happens to my face when I laugh.

'Ah, he means *dimples.*' I say, pointing at the crease beside my mouth.

He roars with laughter and nods his head.

Siling, Dawa and Sarki are sitting across the room from us and Siling asks the lama the name of his gompa.

'*Shaktishali Taksing Gompa,*' the lama replies.

He says this means *Powerful Tiger Lion Gompa.* He tells a story about the statue of Guru Rinpoche, the gompa's founder, which sits inside the gompa beside the statue of Padmasambhava, the founder of Tibetan Buddhism. He says seven people carried the statue over the mountains of Tibet 2,004 years ago. When the people of Lukla and other nearby villages realised they had to come up to such a remote place to venerate the statue, they decided to move it to somewhere more accessible – but the further they carried it down the valley the heavier it became, until eventually they couldn't carry it any longer. When they carried it back up, the statue became lighter until they returned it to its proper place inside Taksing

Gompa.

When Mark and I get up to leave, the lama shakes us each by the hand simultaneously. It's one of those slightly awkward handshakes where the other person doesn't let go. I leave my hand in place until he decides it's time to release it. We continue walking up the trail and hear a whistle behind us. We look back to see that the lama has emerged from the teahouse and is waving goodbye. We leave with a warm feeling. It feels like an auspicious meeting and bodes well for the rest of our journey. Well, I do – and I expect Siling, Dawa and Sarki, who are all Buddhists, do as well – but I'm not so sure about Mark. There seems nothing more natural to me than the lama's cheerful good nature, which I assume comes from a lifetime spent seeking enlightenment in a secluded gompa far from the struggles and complications of the material world. But Mark is sure the reason he kept laughing was because he'd been drinking.

'I notice the monk didn't offer us any of the clear liquid in his own glass,' he mumbles.

It doesn't take us long to walk to Tangnag: about a dozen stone huts with simple camping facilities catering for trekkers. It sits at the top of the Hinku Valley, walled in by the mountains of Kyashar at its head, and Kusum Kangguru and Mera Peak on either side. On the right a steep side valley continues up between Kyashar and Mera Peak – this will be our route of ascent in two days' time after we've rested here for a couple of nights to acclimatise. We're now at an altitude of 4,250m.

The village is situated on a boulder field well above the tree line. It's a bleak spot when the mist descends later in the afternoon, but it's not too cold. We're comfortable enough tucked up in our tents, but I can't help thinking of a story I read about Tangnag.

A few hundred metres above the village there is a glacier lake called Sabai Tsho. In September 1998 an earthquake caused a 100m by 300m section of ice which had been damming the lake to break off. A 2,000m^2 hole was formed, and within ten minutes a deluge filled the Hinku Valley with a ten-metre wall of water, rocks and ice. Smaller floods followed. Within three hours of the dam bursting, the water level had risen to the level of the houses in Tangnag. Miraculously the damage in Tangnag was small. Two houses and three yaks were swept away, and no more casualties were reported, but the effects extended 100km downstream. Bridges and houses were swept away and many people were killed.

Fingers crossed there are no more dams ready to burst.

DAY 8
BOOT TROUBLE

Wednesday, 29 April 2009 – Tangnag, Makalu-Barun National Park, Nepal

There's a busy feel to the village of Tangnag this morning as several large trekking groups pack up for departure to Khare. Our own porters are also going that way today, to complete a load carry of climbing equipment to the higher camps. Mark, Siling, Dawa and I have a rest day. By nine o'clock everybody else has left and we have the village to ourselves.

We decide to go for an acclimatisation walk up the shoulder of nearby Kusum Kangguru. A steep path leads up the hillside above the village, and we begin a long, slow trudge through dwarf rhododendron and juniper. The vegetation thins out to grassland as the hillside tapers to a ridge. Upward we plod. The view east to the Mera Glacier and Mera Peak would be a good appetiser for our climb, but before long we're in a thick, cold mist.

'It's like being in Scotland,' Siling mutters.

Campsite at Tangnag, with Kusum Kangguru
towering overhead

If we exchanged the rhododendron and juniper for bracken and heather then he could be right.

Eventually, hopping up and over boulders, we climb to an altitude of 5,015m where a steep drop abruptly halts our progress. Beyond it the ridge continues up Kusum Kangguru by means of a tall rock tower. The path has long since disappeared and snow flanks the rock tower; above here it becomes a serious rock climb. We turn and head back down again, but not before Dawa surprises us by producing some Snickers and a flask of hot tea. We're back down by 12.30. It's been good acclimatisation.

Unfortunately, I now have some major boot trouble. After trying superglue and gaffer tape to fix a loose bit of leather flapping around on my right boot,

I decided this morning the only way to stop it peeling away any further was to cut the loose bit off with a penknife. But now I've discovered a much more serious problem with my left boot. The whole of the sole has started to tear away. I've cleaned it and lashed it up with gaffer tape, but I'm not sure this will do any good. I've somehow got to make these boots last for another three weeks on rocky trails, and the only alternative – my plastic mountaineering boots designed for rigid crampons on 8,000m peaks – doesn't bear thinking about.

It's with a certain amount of trepidation that I look forward to the following days. I've only had these boots a little over two years, but when I think about it they've done better service than any other boots I've owned. This is their fourth outing to Nepal: they've been around the Annapurna Circuit, up to the arid heights of Naar, Phu and Tilicho, and around the Tamang Heritage Trail. They've taken me up to Advanced Base Camp on the north side of Everest, spent three weeks trekking in Ladakh, and walked to Camp 1 on Muztag Ata. They've also traipsed through bogs in the Rwenzori Mountains, Uganda. Closer to home they've been up nearly thirty Munros in Scotland, up Snowdon twice, and on a great many other weekend hill walks in Wales and the Lake District. This has been a trip too far for them – I can have no complaints. I'm just praying they get me round one last time.

DAY 9
A HIDDEN VALLEY

Thursday, 30 April 2009 – Khare, Makalu-Barun
National Park, Nepal

This morning we have a rocky walk up a glacial stream. It's boulder scrambling to begin with. Then the terrain opens out into a sandy beach and continues steeply on a rough path along the river. Eventually it flattens out at a place called Dig Kharka – a wide plain covered in scrubby grass and rhododendron. The white shelf of the Mera Glacier stretches horizontally ahead on a rock band nearly 1,000m above us, and to our right Mera North rears straight up above the pasture.

Beyond this open space the path turns left up a grassy ridge. Here Siling and I see a small blue bird with a yellowy-orange breast hopping from boulder to boulder.

'It's a blue-fronted redstart,' Siling says, his voice tinged with excitement. Birdwatching is one of his passions.

The path curves back to the right as it ascends into a small basin flanked by huge moraine slopes. Khare, base camp for those attempting Mera Peak, sits within the hollow.

The village comprises a dozen or so trekkers' teahouses set among boulders, with a few rocky terraces built up to form camping pitches. The hollow echoes to the ring of builders' hammers. It's a bit of a dump, but it's home for the next two days while we acclimatise a little more – and it does command a great view back down the valley, with Mera Peak rising up to the left.

From our campsite, Mera North is much the most prominent of Mera Peak's summits, a clear dome of ice rising up at the end of the long snow plateau leading up to it from left to right. This plateau is the Mera Glacier. It will be our ascent route, and I know perfectly well that although it looks like a plateau from Khare, it actually rises at a fairish gradient that will have us puffing and panting when we come to climb it. I have to look pretty hard to make out Mera Central. From here it looks like a tiny pimple on the Mera Glacier just below Mera North. When I stood here five years ago, I was surprised when they told me it was the highest point, but I didn't question it.

Mera Central was first climbed by Jimmy Roberts and Sen Tenzing in 1953. Colonel Jimmy Roberts was an officer in the Gurkha regiment of the British Army, who lived in Nepal for many years and helped to organise the logistics for several expeditions, including Bill Tilman's visit to the Annapurnas in

1950, the 1953 British Everest expedition, and the 1963 American Everest expedition.

Roberts believed that the mountains of Nepal should be accessible not just to elite climbers, but to all lovers of mountains. In 1964 he set up a guiding agency called Mountain Travel Nepal. He advertised a guided trip to the Everest region in the American travel magazine *Holiday* for US$15 a day with all expenses included. Whether it was accident or design that caused him to advertise it as a *trek* rather than the more commonly used *walk* (in the UK) or *hike* (in the US) is not known, but it certainly sounded more exotic, and the word has been used ever since. His first clients were three elderly American ladies. The trip was a success, and Roberts proved that you don't need to be a superman to travel in the Himalayas. I'm sure I'm not the only person who is eternally grateful to him for recognising this.

It probably wasn't any of his expeditions to Everest, Annapurna or Machapuchare that convinced Roberts that Nepal's mountains could be accessible to numpties like me, but his exploratory trip to Mera Peak in 1953.

Mera is one of a small number of mountains that the Nepalese government has designated as *trekking peaks*. This is a slightly misleading term which has led many people to believe they are just treks. Some trekking agencies even advertise Mera as a *walk up*. To all but hardened mountaineers, this is a bit like describing a swim across the English Channel as a *paddle*. All of the trekking peaks require mountaineering skills, and some like Cholatse will test gifted alpine climbers on even their simplest routes.

The term *trekking peak* refers to the paperwork rather than the technical difficulty. You're allowed to climb a trekking peak with little more than a trekking permit, but to climb any other mountain in Nepal, the so-called *expedition peaks*, you need to hire a sirdar and a government liaison officer. Both must be equipped and paid according to an official scale, as do any staff who climb above base camp. This can be prohibitively expensive if there are only one or two climbers, and most expeditions need to have several members sharing the costs, making logistics more complicated as well. To add insult to injury, corruption is rife and most liaison officers are no more likely to show up than Lord Lucan. The majority of liaison officers pocket their fee and remain in Kathmandu.

Roberts made the first ascent of Mera Peak on 20 May 1953. With him on the summit was Sen Tenzing, a Sherpa who had accompanied many of the British Everest expeditions of the 1930s and had been given the nickname *The Foreign Sportsman* on account of his flamboyant dress sense.

Roberts had been helping with the logistics for 1953 British Everest expedition that eventually put Edmund Hillary and Tenzing Norgay on the summit. But his service to the expedition ended when his porters delivered the final load of supplies to their depot at Tengboche. From that moment on, everything that happened higher up the trail became the responsibility of expedition leader Brigadier John Hunt, and Roberts was free to leave.

We of the tail of the British Everest Expedition reached Thyangboche [Tengboche] and I was thankful to hand over the oxygen loads. I now had about six weeks to roam, explore, and climb as the spirit might move me.

In this sentence from his official account of the expedition, you can feel the sense of anticipation he must have felt. He chose to explore the area directly south of Tengboche, because it was an area that neither Tilman nor Eric Shipton had explored in their few reconnaissance trips since Nepal opened its borders in 1949.

One of his Sherpas, Dhanu, came from the village of Chaunrikharka, a day's walk down the valley from Namche. Dhanu said that he knew of a pleasant yak pasture surrounded by high peaks. It was two days' walk over a high ridge above his village. Chaunrikharka is the first village trekkers pass through when they leave Lukla on the Everest Base Camp trail. This was long before Hillary had bought the land for the airport. The 'ridge' Dhanu was referring to is the Zatr La, a high pass directly above Lukla. I crossed this pass on my way back from Mera Peak in 2004. Roberts, Sen Tenzing and their porters crossed it in the other direction, arriving above the pine forests of the Hinku Valley and descending to a place that must have been close to where the village of Kote now stands.

Roberts was thrilled to discover that the Hinku Valley contained a river as substantial as any in the Khumbu region to the north. This meant that somewhere in its upper reaches there must be a substantial glacier system feeding it. At this point, they would have seen the regal crown of Mera's three summits rising nearly 3,000m above them.

Two days later, they had skirted the west and north sides of the mountain, and were standing on the Mera La, just 1,000m below the summit. From here they could see the straightforward ascent up the Mera Glacier that I was looking at now. Roberts described Mera from that angle as, 'an indeterminate, rambling sort of a mountain' with a 'mass of false summits'. He too was having trouble deciding which was the highest.

He could see there was a considerable horizontal distance to cover, but there were no real technical difficulties. They went off to explore the Hinku Glacier basin, a broad plateau of converging glaciers. This lies over a ridge to the north of Khare. It turned out to be the glacier system they had been looking for as the source of the substantial Hinku Khola river. They climbed a couple of high passes and looked down into Tengboche's Imja Valley, thus completing a blank on their map. Then they returned to climb Mera. They reached the summit of Mera Central, but Roberts believed that Mera North, rising a short distance away, might be a little higher.

The summit ridge, running from west to east,
consists of three or four large bumps and we chose
the eastern one. To our west a semi-detached wave of
ice hanging over the southern precipices may have
been about 100 feet higher.

After climbing Mera, the party descended the Mera La into the Hongu Valley to the east, where they found Dhanu's pleasant yak pasture. We will be trekking up this valley ourselves on our way to the Amphu Labtsa, and I'm very much looking forward to it.

Jimmy Roberts is generally regarded as the grandfather of trekking in Nepal. He wasn't the first person to lead commercial treks and climbs of Mera Peak, but this little reconnaissance of his, an insignificant postscript to the giant media story that was the first ascent of Everest, may well have sowed the seeds of commercial trekking in his mind.

After lunch, Mark, Siling and I walk up a ridge above the village to an altitude of 5,150m. At the top, it looks like previous visitors have been competing to build the most precariously balanced cairn. There are dozens of them; we feel compelled to build a few of our own. Siling tells us it's auspicious to build in multiples of three. We manage to get to six stones high before they all collapse. Back home in the UK, some hikers get upset about people building unnecessary cairns. Taken to excess I can see what they mean, but up here in this remote location, with a seemingly infinite supply of rocks all around, it feels pretty harmless. You can always push them over if you don't like it.

The sky has started to cloud over a little, but otherwise the view from the top is magnificent. We look down upon a huge hanging valley at about 4,500m, completely hidden from Khare by the moraine. Glaciers tumble from giant peaks whose summits rise up into cloud. Vast hummocks of lateral moraine frame each side of the valley, suggesting there was once a huge glacier spilling down towards the village. This is the Hinku Glacier basin that Jimmy Roberts discovered in 1953, that is the ultimate source of much of the water in the Hinku Valley.

I believe I'm looking at the backside of Ama Dablam. Siling tells me I'm wrong, but he can't tell me the name of the impressive three-pronged mountain that rises above the far side of the basin.

On our way back down we pass a group of elderly Japanese slogging up to the viewpoint. They all look to be in their 70s and are struggling on what should be an easy stroll. One man in orange keeps stopping to lean on his sticks every few metres. When I pass him, he is motionless and breathing with difficulty. If they are planning on climbing Mera Peak then it seems very unlikely they will succeed. By contrast our much younger French-Canadian friend – who has never been to this altitude before – skips past them.

Back at camp, Mark and I are sorting out our gear in the tent when Mark's friend Ade comes over. He's leading a trekking group for the UK company KE

Adventure Travel. Our merry band of porters are laughing as he sits outside the porch talking to us. They think he must be Mark's brother – over the last few days of trekking both of them have grown beards tinged with grey streaks.

'As long as they don't call me *Bhaje*,' Ade says, a little grumpily. 'I've been called that a few times here.'

'What, as in onion *bhaji*?' I ask. 'The dish you get in curry houses.'

'*Bhaje*, not *bhaji*,' he replies. 'It means grandad.'

I reassure Ade that he looks positively youthful compared with the Japanese group we saw.

DAY 10
ONTO THE MERA GLACIER

Friday, 1 May 2009 – Khare, Makalu-Barun National Park,
Nepal

I've discovered a hidden mountain no one knows about. It's called Malangphulang and it's 6,573m high – surprisingly tall for a mountain nobody seems to have noticed.

Wedged between Ama Dablam, Kangtega and Peak 41, apparently it's not visible from the Everest trail, and it can only be seen from the south side if you climb above Khare on an acclimatisation walk. In fact, it's the very mountain I thought might be Ama Dablam yesterday, but isn't. I described its position precisely to all the Nepalis in the lodge last night, including the trekking old stagers Siling, Dawa and Sarki, but nobody knew its name. Some of them seem to think I invented it, but now I've got photos and a map as evidence.

We wake up this morning to several inches of fresh snow. The porters are finding my gaffer-taped boots hilarious. I ask the cheekiest of them, Drukchen (also known as the *Little Dragon*, a translation of his name into English), if he's willing to swap them for his flip-flops, but he's not having any of it.

Figures pass in front of Malangphulang (6,573m),
the secret mountain

We're supposed to have a rest day today. As often happens on expedition 'rest days', we end up slogging our way up a hill. In this case, we go all the way up a glacier to the Mera La.

We start with a slow plod up the hillside above Khare to the base of the Mera Glacier. The bulk of the glacier sits on a horizontal shelf spanning the Mera La, but in order to get onto the flat section we have to find a way up a steep crevassed bit of old rotten ice about 200m high. We only need to climb about 50m of steep ice if we scramble up rocks alongside it, but Dawa decides we should do it the hard way and climb up from the very bottom.

As we're getting our boots, crampons and harnesses on at the foot of the ice, Ade turns up with his KE group to do the same thing – and he decides to get some tour-operator banter going.

'How do I get a Responsible Travellers fleece, then?' he says to Siling with a smirk when he sees both he and Dawa wearing fleeces which bear the name of Siling's trekking company.

'Well, you have to be responsible for a start,' Mark says, 'so I think you're fucked.'

Then he notices our climbing equipment has been packed into a blue KE duffle bag which has gaffer tape stuck over the logo and the words *The Responsible Travellers* written across it in marker pen. It's an old bag of Mark's that he was given when he signed up for a KE trek many years ago. We decided to modify it for Siling's benefit.

Ade frowns. 'I'm not sure I should be letting you use that bag.'

'But it's a Responsible Travellers bag,' I reply. 'Can't you see?'

'Actually, I told them we shouldn't have put the tape on it,' Mark says. 'Then we could have got one of your porters to carry it up for us.'

Dawa, Siling, Mark and I rope together and start up the glacier at an angle of about 45°, zigzagging up old pinnacles of wind-blown ice. It's tiring work at this altitude. The ice is hard and crusty, making it difficult to drive our crampons in for a firm foothold, but we take it slowly and without any major difficulties. Towards the top we come across porters walking up the shorter path with heavy loads and without the benefit of crampons. This makes me feel like a bit of a tit.

At the top Dawa produces another flask of tea and some Mars bars. By now the weather has closed in and visibility is poor. We walk for about twenty minutes along a snow plateau to the Mera La, where the summit route continues upwards and a path drops away to the left, to the bleak Mera La campsite set among rocks just beneath the glacier. Here, at 5,350m, we turn around and head back to camp. It may not be much of a rest day, but it's good acclimatisation.

Back at camp we have more snow and spend most of the afternoon sheltering in our tents.

DAY 11
THE MERA LA

Saturday, 2 May 2009 – Mera La, Makalu-Barun
National Park, Nepal

We have a lazy day today. The sky is a beautiful clear blue when I get up this morning, and word is that there will be congestion at the Mera La campsite later. As well as ourselves and the KE group with their eleven clients, a Jagged Globe group of sixteen clients is due to head for the summit today. They intend to stay at the Mera La on their way down. Through binoculars from Khare we can just make out figures – which could be them – creeping up to the dome of Mera's central summit.

We leave Khare shortly after eight o'clock and climb up onto the ridge above the village. Not only is my hidden mountain Malangphulang visible to the north, but we can see a full horseshoe spanning the Mera Glacier and the route up to Mera's summits across a bowl beneath the ridge.

We repeat the slow plod of yesterday up grassy

paths, then gravelly scree, to the foot of the Mera Glacier. Eschewing the direct route straight up the glacier's snout onto the plateau, this time we scramble up boulders to the right, giving us an easier and shorter ascent up the steep, broken part of the glacier. Here Dawa, Siling, Mark and I don plastic boots and crampons, and rope up to climb above the main walking route. We pass one of our younger porters, Pemba, cutting steps with an ice axe that Dawa has leant him. A line of porters from other groups follows him.

I'm dismayed to discover that my Scarpa Phantom 8000 climbing boots are causing discomfort and tearing up my right heel on the steeper sections. Apart from yesterday, I've only worn them once before, on Chulu Far East last autumn, and I'm relying on them to take me up and down Gasherbrum in the summer.

I've had problems with brand new plastic boots in the past; I can only hope I'm able to find a comfortable solution in time. I'm not having much luck with boots on this expedition. These ones appear to be too loose, so I'll be trying extra socks tomorrow. I mention my problem to Mark when we reach camp – he doesn't seem concerned. He says feet will expand at the higher altitudes on Gasherbrum, and it's better for the boots to be too loose than too tight. This is all very well for him to say; he doesn't have to wear them.

We reach the Mera La campsite at eleven o'clock. By now the clouds have closed in and it feels like a bleak, damp spot, as it was last time I stayed here in 2004. It's situated on a rocky shelf just below the glacier pass. Pools of water ripple in the breeze. Piles of trash from previous expeditions lurk among the rubble. On a clear day there will be fine views from here, but today there are just the gloomy whites and greys of an unknown rocky mountain across the valley from us. It looks even more grim on the route above us, which continues up the Mera Glacier. Visibility is down to just a few metres.

Mark and I stay in our tent all afternoon as we listen to the snow pounding on the roof. There is no question of heading up the glacier for an acclimatisation walk. The kitchen crew serve us lunch and tea at the porch of our tent, and our only dilemma in the afternoon is whether to use pee bottles or head out into the drizzly snow. To avoid complete vegetative laziness, we opt for the latter in the optimistic hope that there may be a view emerging from the gloom outside. There never is.

DAY 12
A GLORIOUS PLACE TO CAMP

Sunday, 3 May 2009 – Mera Peak, Makalu-Barun
National Park, Nepal

I write this sitting on a rock shelf thousands of metres up, with views across to some of the highest mountains on Earth. High camp on Mera Peak is an amazing setting, but last time I was here I remember finding it a bit bleak. I spent most of the few hours I stayed here cooped up in my tent with a banging headache. Not so this time.

We set off from the Mera La campsite at about 8.30 this morning. The four of us in the summit party – myself, Mark, Siling and Dawa – are roped together, and we complete our slow plod up the glacier, an ascent of around 500m, in less than two hours.

As we ascend, directly behind us and towering over the Mera La, is a prominent rock peak which nobody has ever been able to find a name for. It's still known as Peak 41, a relic from the 19th century Survey of India, when peaks were initially given numbers until a local name could be found. For a reason known only to itself, for over thirty years the Nepal Mountaineering Association (NMA), custodian of Nepal's trekking peaks, has listed the height of this mountain, 6,654m, as the official height of Mera Peak. I don't know how many NMA guides have been up Mera – it's likely to be hundreds – but it seems that none of them have ever been tempted to clear up this little error by carrying a GPS. Mera Peak is clearly nowhere near this height, but in a scenario reminiscent of W.E. Bowman's comic novel *The Ascent of Rum Doodle* – where most of the team end up climbing the wrong mountain – this has led a small handful of people who have climbed the much harder Peak 41 to call it the *Real Mera Peak*. They claim, presumably tongue-in-cheek, that the rest of us have been up the wrong one. Apart from the flimsy evidence of an inexplicable thirty-year typo, there's no reason to suppose that Mera Peak isn't the real Mera.

We share some of the climb with the quick rope from Ade's KE group, two women and one man, which must dent the pride of some of the gentlemen in the team. They're much faster than the rest of their group. We keep changing places with them in tortoise-and-hare fashion – they overtake us, but then we plod past them again when they stop for a rest.

We hardly stop at all. Dawa maintains a steady pace throughout, and we reach camp a little ahead of them, though not much. I can tell there's been very little snow over the last few weeks. The path up the glacier is completely clear. The route from the Mera

La is gentle at first before gradually steepening, with a few small crevasses to dodge as we approach high camp. We complete most of the ascent in light snow and poor visibility.

High camp is perched on a rocky shelf, sheltering behind a large vertical rock that shields the area to an extent. There is only space for a handful of tents and today it's pretty much full, though Mark and I have the king of pitches at the top of the shelf, overlooking everyone else. As we're settling down we hear the familiar voices of two trekkers, James and Rosie, outside the tent – one English, the other Northern Irish. We shared a lodge with them in the evenings at both Tangnag and Khare. They've just returned from the summit and are about to head back to Khare.

We congratulate them and enquire about conditions. The young whippersnapper James is in great shape. He says they were on the summit early enough to have clear views above the cloud we must have been walking through. I know from experience this is one of the best views in the world. Rosie returns my copy of Wilfrid Noyce's *Climbing the Fish's Tail*, which I gave her to read in Khare, not expecting to see it again. She's finished it already. It's a splendid little book about an expedition to Machapuchare in the Annapurna region of Nepal – an expedition that was led by the very same Jimmy Roberts who made the first ascent of Mera Peak.

The snow continues for an hour or so, then clears all of a sudden. I rush out of the tent with my camera and take a video panorama. Below our little shelf, a wide expanse of snow and ice angles down to the Hongu Valley 1,000m below, our next destination after Mera. A line of crinkled, fluted peaks stretches from right to left on the skyline, culminating in the impressive Chamlang, rising to 7,319m: a narrow disc rammed vertically into the landscape, so distinctive that it was the only mountain I felt confident of identifying as we flew in to Lukla a week ago.

Two lakes nestle in the Hongu Valley at the foot of Chamlang's vertical wall – one blue and one green – and behind the mountain's northern shoulder rises 8,463m Makalu, the fifth-highest mountain in the world. Very little snow covers its slopes. From this angle it's a perfect dark rock pyramid.

Above us the summits of Mera Peak stretch in a wave of white lumps. The first lump is a steeper section that we'll have to walk behind. The second is the little nipple – more of a breast now that we're closer – that marks Mera's central summit, the peak most people go for and the one I climbed five years ago. The whaleback hump of the northern summit rises to the right: this is the peak we'll be aiming for tomorrow if conditions are good.

Sarki provides us with some lunch. I sit outside our tent eating and admiring the view, but before I've finished, the sun has evaporated much of the snow below us, and a wave of clouds has risen up from the valley to hide the summits again.

The afternoon passes lazily. Ade comes to our tent for a bit of banter. Although the tourist route up Mera is an easy (if tiring) snow slog up a glacier, other routes are far from straightforward: the summits are guarded by huge rock faces, great waves of snow seracs and cornices. Throughout the day we're intermittently bombarded by loud cracks and rustles as another avalanche sweeps down from one of Mera's faces.

'Apparently Doug Scott once tried to climb the south face of Mera,' Ade says, 'but was forced to turn back before he reached the summit.'

'Yeah, but that was only because he ran out of fags,' Mark quips.

He appears to be confusing Doug Scott with Don Whillans, another great British climber of the 1960s and 1970s, who was famous for his uncompromising lifestyle of cigarettes and alcohol. Likewise, I don't know whether Ade's story about Mera Peak defeating the great Doug Scott is true. I do know that Doug Scott made a first ascent of the north summit of Kusum Kangguru, as well as several ascents of Chamlang, a much bigger mountain. Perhaps Ade is mistaking one of these, though the story is plausible.

Later in the afternoon it's time for me to brave *turd corner*. The rock shelf angles downwards, and around the corner of the tower there is a section of ledge hidden from the tents. I remember sneaking round this corner to answer the call of nature five years ago, only to find the area laden with frozen turds. The experience wasn't pleasant and I'm now forced to repeat it.

To my surprise, mine are the only footprints in the snow leading to this secluded spot. Everybody else has been using an area above the camp, and recent visitors have all had the decency to cover their stools with a rock. It's a most pleasant diversion crouching down with fine views of Makalu and Chamlang. My only fear is lifting a rock to bury my business and uncovering another fresh turd – which wouldn't be a new experience for me.

'Job done,' Mark says when I return to the tent.

Looking up towards Mera Peak's summits, with Mera North on the right and Mera Central visible as a pimple on the skyline to its left

Just before dusk the sky clears again. Kangchenjunga, 120km away on the Indian border and the third-highest mountain in the world, appears perfectly framed in a gap between two mountains from the door of our tent. Siling, Mark and I watch the sunset from the glacier just above high camp as the sun drops behind a huge panorama to the north that includes Cho Oyu, Everest, Lhotse and Makalu, four more of the world's six highest mountains.

Meanwhile Dawa has an unexpected trip up the glacier to rescue a kitchen boy from one of the other groups. The lad fancied his chances on Mera Peak and fell down a crevasse a couple of hundred metres above camp. Without ice axe or crampons he was unable to climb out on his own, but fortunately he didn't fall far. He is pulled out unharmed – and before he's had time to become hypothermic – but the Nepalis in camp are quite embarrassed about the incident.

DAY 13
A TRIO OF SUMMITS

Monday, 4 May 2009 – Mera Peak, Makalu-Barun National Park, Nepal

Our wake-up call for Mera Peak summit day comes at 2am. I rise with a throbbing headache and take an aspirin with my tea. Mark and I got most of our kit ready last night, so we're able to put all of it on inside the tent, except our crampons. Although Gombu, one of the kitchen assistants, appears in the porch with hard-boiled eggs and chapati, neither of us can eat and we leave our plates on top of our sleeping bags inside the tent.

Thankfully, once we're on our feet and out of the tent, my headache disappears and does not return. We set off at three o'clock, the four of us roped together with Dawa at the front, me behind because I'm the slowest and he can use me to regulate his pace, then Mark, with Siling at the back. Ahead we see head torches of climbers who have set off before us, but we soon overtake them and find ourselves on our own up front.

For two hours, we plod slowly up steep featureless snow in the dark. We don't stop for the first hour or so, but when the slope steepens and I feel myself beginning to tire, I ask Dawa to halt and we take on some water. I have my bottle stuffed down the front of my down jacket to stop it freezing and to provide easy access. Dawa continues on his way, occasionally probing the snow in front of him with his walking pole when he thinks there might be a crevasse – and there are a few, but most are small and we can easily step over, keeping the rope tight between us. As the slope continues and Dawa trudges onwards without stopping, I keep going in reasonable comfort by taking a deep breath with every step. Only once or twice do I need to ask him to stop for a longer break.

At 5.15 the orange of dawn breathes light onto the line of mountains behind us. I stop for a photo of Everest and Makalu, but it's still very cold and it takes a few minutes for my fingers to warm up again. Now we're approaching the summit plateau. First we see the trekking summit rising above the line of snow above us. This is the highest point on the mountain that doesn't require any technical climbing to reach its top. It's sufficiently distinctive to be considered a summit, if barely. It's the place where trekking groups take the clients who decide that the central summit is beyond them. We walk a little further, and at last, more dramatically, we see the twin mounds of Mera Central and Mera North linked by a short corniced ridge. Nearly everyone who climbs Mera Peak climbs the central summit believing they have reached the highest point, and don't give Mera North a second glance.

This is what I did in 2004. I arrived at the summit freezing cold and exhausted. In the dark, I didn't even notice Mera North was there, never mind how close to Mera Central it was. But this time it has been our plan to try and climb Mera North – all the most recent maps show it to be slightly higher. Ideally we'd like to climb both summits and measure their respective altitudes with a GPS, but we don't have any idea of the conditions on Mera North, or whether it's even possible to climb – so few people have climbed it that no one could give us any information.

Approaching Mera Peak's two principal summits: Mera Central (left, 6,461m) and Mera North (right, 6,476m)

Now we have both summits to ourselves and are faced with a choice. Mera Central looks slightly higher as we approach, but it's also nearer. From the foot of its dome a corniced section leads to the adjacent top of Mera North, and there is clearly no route beneath the cornice, where a huge crevasse beneath the ridge guards the summit. Our hope lies in a safe route on the ridge behind the overhanging cornice. From there a crevasse-free slope leads up to the top, though it looks steep and daunting.

'What do you want to do, guys?' I ask between deep breaths.

Mark's answer is immediate: 'North. Well – preferably both.'

This settles it. Dawa leads the way forward beneath the central summit and over a lip that leads onto the ridge behind the cornice. It looks good. Beyond the lip the ridge angles away slowly, but it's wide enough to enable safe passage well beneath the cornice, to avoid any danger of it collapsing beneath our weight. Once we have traversed the ridge, the steep slope up the summit dome is our only obstacle – from here at least, it looks do-able. The slope is steep, and only a little beneath it is the sheer cliff of Mera's south face, but there seems to be a reasonable layer of snow, allowing us to arrest with our axes in the event of a fall. Even better, the sun has only just risen. Although the cornice is receiving its full glare, the ridge and slope onto the summit are still in shadow, vastly reducing the risk of the snow collapsing beneath us and triggering a mini avalanche.

Dawa doesn't hesitate. Within a few minutes we've traversed the ridge and are standing beneath the snow slope. He extends the length of rope between himself and me to about 20m, and slowly begins working his way up the slope, stamping steps with his crampons for me to follow. He has lengthened the rope so that if the snow gives way beneath him and avalanches, the rest of us are sufficiently far behind not to be carried with it. Between the three of us we should be able to hold his fall. Similarly, if the snow collapses beneath us, he'll stand a better chance of holding all three of us.

The slope proves to be safe. I follow in Dawa's footprints, keeping the rope tight between us and ramming my ice axe firmly into the snow above me with each step. At approximately 6.30am we're standing on the summit of Mera North. Only a handful of other climbers have ever been here.

The humped dome hides a broad summit plateau, which we have to ourselves – none of the climbers behind us will be following us up here. It's strange that everyone ignores this summit, and if it proves to be higher than Mera Central then it seems wrong that none of the big trekking companies who take their clients up Mera Central ever tell them they're not climbing the true summit of the mountain.

We take many pictures. I get out my GPS to take a waypoint and measure the altitude. As it finds more and more satellites it homes in on the mark recorded on more recent maps: 6,476m.

The view to the north, of Cho Oyu, Kangtega,

Nuptse, Everest, Lhotse, Makalu, Chamlang and many smaller peaks, is clear and breathtaking. A huge human-shaped shadow lies across the south face of Cho Oyu, and I tell Siling it must be the shadow of a yeti. Nuptse is not so much a summit from this angle, but a black ridge of jagged rock, crowned on its right-hand end by Lhotse. The black pyramid of Everest rises behind this wall, clearly higher than everything else. It's a classic view of Everest that appears on many photographs, though probably not from this precise viewpoint.

Beneath us we see a line of trekkers approaching the base of Mera Central – dozens of them – and yet we have this summit to ourselves.

Feeling pleased with ourselves, we leave to descend at seven o'clock. In next to no time we're down the snow slope and across the ridge. As we approach the base of Mera Central, Siling, who is now leading, looks back.

'Shall we climb this one as well?'

The response from me and Mark is emphatic: 'Of course.'

Some Sherpas from the KE group are fixing a rope up the summit dome. Yesterday Ade told us we were welcome to use their ropes if we wanted, but as three of his clients wait beneath us, Siling sneaks in ahead of them; first Mark goes up, then Siling, then me, then Dawa. The ascent is steeper than Mera North, hence the fixed rope, but also safer because there is no risk of the snow giving way beneath us. I attach my jumar (a safety device that locks onto the rope in the event of a fall) to the rope with my right hand. I steady myself with my ice axe in my left. The slope is very steep, 60° or more, and no steps have been cut by preceding climbers, so the only way up is by front-pointing my crampons into the slope – this puts a heavy strain on the backs of my calves. I gradually make my way up the 30m to the summit plateau. Shortly before reaching the top, I look up to see Mark and Siling pointing their cameras at me. Then I flop onto the summit plateau, exhausted, and need a few seconds to get my breath back.

Like Mera North, Mera Central's dome hides a broad flat plateau. This one seems to be a bit smaller, though this may simply be because it's also more crowded. Although the view is much the same as from Mera North, it's great to have climbed both peaks, and satisfying to look back across at the north peak and see our footprints leading up the steep slope to the summit.

It's still only 7.30 and I take out my GPS to measure the altitude again. From here, Mera North looks slightly higher, and the GPS confirms the recorded altitude of 6,461m. We've now firmly established which summit is higher by our own observations. Only today, four and a half years after I first came here, can I truly say I've climbed it. It also means that the first true ascent of Mera Peak wasn't made by Jimmy Roberts and Sen Tenzing in 1953, but probably by a team of French climbers in the 1970s using the same route we have taken ourselves.

Only three of Ade's clients decide to climb the fixed

rope onto Mera Central, and from the summit we can see a rope length of the rest of them making their way up to the trekking summit, a small hillock to our east. It doesn't surprise me that most of the KE group have settled for this option. Trekking brochures often describe Mera as 'one of Nepal's highest walk-up peaks'; clients would therefore be surprised to discover they have to get on a rope and climb.

Although it's only an insignificant hummock compared with the steep domes of Mera North and Mera Central, Mark and I decide that we might as well walk up there and round off our successful morning by completing the set. We abseil off the summit dome and meet our French-Canadian friend at the bottom. He's just been up there himself, and for someone who's never been to high altitude before, he's done amazingly well. We complete our trio of ascents by walking up to the trekking summit (which I measure as 6,431m on my GPS). We take some quick photos of the two main summit domes before a brisk descent to high camp, which we reach at 9.30, six and a half hours after setting out.

The weather has been fine all morning, but about 100m above high camp we enter a thick mist that remains for the rest of the day. We have a brief rest and some tea. We discover that Sarki has cooked us some spaghetti bolognese, which I'm sorry to say I find very difficult to eat at 9.30 in the morning. Then we pack up the tents before descending further. I'm very slow at this operation, and everyone is waiting for me. The porters start taking our tent down while

I'm still inside it, and Dawa tries to help me take off my harness, which is a bit embarrassing – mainly when he struggles to undo the waist buckle with his fingers and decides to use his teeth instead. Fortunately nobody seems to be watching, or they might get the wrong idea.

We leave to descend at eleven o'clock. High camp is deserted now – it appears to be the end of the season – and we meet just one lone girl and her guide coming up. We reach the Mera La camp at midday. It's still as bleak as hell. Every time I've been here it seems to be engulfed in a thick grey mist. My plastic mountaineering boots have ripped my ankles to shreds, and it's a joy to change back into my walking boots again, even though they're falling apart. We hastily pack up our things at the Mera La camp and continue our descent behind Dawa.

For all I know the next hour and a half may be the most picturesque part of the entire trek, but for most of it visibility is little more than 10m. We appear to descend into a gravelly valley to begin with, then we spend about half an hour rock hopping up and down with a cliff to our left and (I think) a drop to our right. The terrain is less than comfortable. Short steep uphill sections are unexpected and painful on my shredded heels, but eventually we meet grassy moorland and it becomes more comfortable underfoot as the trail continues to descend. We could be in Scotland again for all I can see of the scenery. Eventually the mist clears a little and we can see a broad valley with a single hut beneath us, which I assume must be a campsite.

After crossing a few stony river beds, we reach camp at Kongme Dingma at two o'clock, after eleven hours of walking and a great deal of ascent and descent. It's been a very successful day, but I'm exhausted.

Half an hour later Mark and I both find ourselves nodding off in our tent, and the next we know Siling is calling for dinner. It's 5.30 and three hours have disappeared.

We're not the only tired people. As we eat our dinner in the mess tent, one of the porters, Pemba, is curled up in his sleeping bag in the corner. He has about an hour's peace and quiet as we eat, but when we leave, his seven comrades pile in, and it's hard to believe he'll sleep through it. Our heads hit our pillows at seven o'clock and I must be asleep immediately. It's been a long day.

DAY 14
THE HONGU VALLEY

Tuesday, 5 May 2009 – Hongu Valley, Makalu-Barun
National Park, Nepal

'Good morning, sir.'

Groggily, I come to and notice that Gombu's grinning face has appeared at the door of the tent. He's bearing tea.

I've slept through twelve hours without any difficulty. Outside it's a fine day, and now I can see we're in a wide green valley walled in by hillsides rippling with grass. We came down one of the hillsides yesterday afternoon. I realise that we must be camped in the fabled yak pasture that Jimmy Roberts went looking for fifty years ago. The only snow-capped peak I can see is an outlier of Peak 41 up a side valley, but I know from our view this way from high camp on Mera Peak two days ago that we're surrounded by high mountains hiding behind the hills.

We leave camp shortly after eight o'clock, and

immediately begin climbing one of the hillsides around a corner into the main Hongu Valley. When we reach the corner about 50m higher up, the view that greets us causes my heart to flutter with excitement. It's truly stunning. The giant 7,319m peak of Chamlang rises up across the valley beyond a small green lake. I don't forget to look behind me, where a new angle to Mera Peak displays itself above the grassy hill we came down yesterday.

Its multi-summit profile is still just as distinctive. From where we stand it's clear that its three main summits are the three we climbed yesterday. All maps mark an apparently insignificant point on Mera's eastern ridge 400m below the main summits as Mera South, but from this angle the trekking summit is far more prominent and should be more properly described as the third summit of Mera Peak.[1]

Our porters are taking a rest on the bank above the lake, looking towards Chamlang. It makes for a good photo – but just as I produce my camera Mark moves in front of them with his own camera and shouts, 'Smile'. He's spotted the view of Mera Peak behind us, and they all cheer and pose for his photo instead of mine.

1

In fact this is only true from where I stand; had I looked behind me later in the day from higher up the Hongu Valley, Mera South would have been much more obviously a separate peak

Above the lake we pass Ade's KE group. The next couple of hours' walking are my favourite of the trek so far. The top end of the Hongu Valley is a significant contrast to the Hinku Valley that we came up last week: while the latter is narrow, and completely enclosed by forest except thousands of metres above its base, this one is wide and open, with bouldery slopes of grass and prominent snow-capped mountains visible at regular intervals. Chamlang is there on our right all the time.

We start by traversing high above the left side of the valley, but soon drop down to the valley floor. Here, wide pebbled shores are dappled with boulders and grassy hummocks, and I amble along, thoroughly enjoying this part of the trek. Later I hear a shout behind me – Siling has caught up, and he points out the line of mountains straight ahead up the valley. To the left is a jagged black wall holding very little snow. Behind it, there is a prominent black rock pyramid.

'Do you recognise it?' he asks.

I didn't, but now he's drawn my attention to it, it's obvious: the jagged wall is Lhotse, and the black pyramid can only be Everest.

We stop for lunch at a junction of valleys. The kitchen crew have laid out the blue tarpaulin and roll mats in a sheltered spot surrounded by stone walls. They serve us cinnamon rolls for lunch, but Siling complains that because he always eats with us, he never seems to get the Nepali favourite of *dal bhat* (rice and lentils) like everyone else.

We discuss future projects, as we often have on this

expedition. This time we talk about a long trek in the far west of Nepal, from warm and secluded Rara Lake, north across the border into Tibet and culminating in the pilgrims' circuit of Mount Kailash. None of us have seen this most arresting of peaks, the holiest mountain in Buddhism – and we all want to.

'This will be a month-long trek,' Siling says, 'and the *kora* [circuit of Mount Kailash] will be about eight days.'

'Siling will be doing prostrations,' I tell Mark, 'so it will take him longer.'

As its name implies, this involves prostrating yourself on your face and stomach all the way along the trail rather than just walking. Although it sounds absurd to westerners, hundreds of devout Buddhist and Hindu pilgrims – all of whom regard Mount Kailash as sacred – do it every year.

'Can't you lie face down on a wheeled sledge and get someone to tow you?' Mark says.

I nod. 'Good idea. In all the years pilgrims have been doing the *kora*, I'm amazed no one's thought of this.'

Siling lets out a nervous giggle. I don't know whether he's shocked or just thoughtful.

As we talk, a weird mist drifts up the valley from below and quickly obscures the surrounding peaks. It's the thinnest of thin mists; although we can't see any of the landscape around us, the sun streams right through it and our sheltered spot remains warm. I'm concerned it will thicken and be followed by the rains we had for most of yesterday.

I turn to Siling. 'Is this the pattern in these parts? After a beautiful morning, is it now going to turn into weather like yesterday?'

'I'm afraid that might be so,' he replies.

But for once, thankfully, he's wrong. For the first hour after lunch we trudge up and down through the mist, not as bad as yesterday, but obscuring any views there might be. We seem to be stuck with the KE group and their army of porters now. I frequently find myself plodding along behind a whole line of them – which destroys the feeling of remoteness and solitude I relished this morning. Worse, my comfy boots are rubbing acutely on the backs of my heels, particularly on steep uphill sections. I contemplate the six months of travels I have ahead of me, which I've been looking forward to for a while. All of it involves walking up steep hills. When will my feet have a chance to heal – or will I have to put up with this rubbing in my boots for six months?

We come over a rock brow, and ahead is a wide sandy beach framing one edge of a small white lake. As though beaches have power to control the sun, all of a sudden the mist dissipates and the sun beats down. Across the lake, the now-familiar black ramparts of Everest and Lhotse rise up like a citadel. Siling tells me the lake is called *Sete Pokhara* or *White Lake*. It's only a small lake and much of it is covered by a thin film of ice, but it's a bizarre experience. Here I am at 5,000m, standing on a beach, looking up at Everest.

I forget the pain in my heels for two hours as I

walk alongside the lake and into tussock meadows behind. I can't stop taking pictures. Now the once-despised porters form great foreground subject matter for my photos, walking the trail with the mountains up ahead of them. It's one of those afternoons when past and future are forgotten and I find myself living for the present only, so lucky do I feel to be experiencing such a beautiful landscape.

Porters crossing a beach, with the wall of Lhotse in cloud

We camp in a wider part of the valley covered by an expanse of uneven tussock grass. Trickling streams meander through. A large boulder slope dwarfs the regular campsite. Dawa is walking ahead with Mark, and he takes an executive decision to camp on a flatter section of grass on the opposite side, where the slopes above are gentler and the rocks are not so precarious.

The KE group follow suit, and soon a small village of tents has arisen.

In the evening the porters light a fire and our boys and theirs gather round, mingling freely. Again a person is curled up in a sleeping bag in the corner of our mess tent when we take dinner this evening. This time it's Temba – the quiet one, slightly older than the others – and he doesn't move. By seven o'clock the fire has died out and his companions appear at the door of the tent, crowding in for some warmth. It's time for us to head for the shelter of our own tent and sleeping bags.

DAY 15
HIGH LAKES

Wednesday, 6 May 2009 – Panch Pokhari, Makalu-Barun National Park, Nepal

It's another of those days when all concerns are forgotten and everything seems right with the world. Life seems so simple when I am passing through such breathtaking scenery, and it's impossible to take pleasure like this for granted.

There's a short three-and-a-half-hour walk up to our high camp at 5,400m, beneath the Amphu Labtsa pass. We ascend above the tussock grass and pass a series of small lakes. Soon we're walking on top of the lateral moraine of a glacier, and the black castle of Everest and Lhotse is replaced by the dramatic white expanse of Kali Himal and Baruntse, a 7,129m mountain that Dawa has climbed. He describes the route he took up it as we look across a grey glacier lake 100m below the trail.

We amble slowly, stopping often. 'Great choice, mate,' I say to Mark at one point.

'What's that?'

'Suggesting we do this trek as our Gasherbrum warm-up.'

The sun is fierce all morning, but when we crest a brow and emerge onto a broad plateau occupied by the final lake, the wind hits us and it's suddenly very cold. The icy blast is only brief. We work our way around to a more sheltered spot.

Mark, Siling and I discuss the definition of 'highest lake in the world'. All three of us were together at Tilicho Lake in the Annapurna region six months ago. A national park sign at one end of the lake described it as, you guessed it, *the highest lake in the world*, and I have video footage of Mark ranting on about what you define as a lake. Tilicho is at 4,900m, but here we are at 5,400m, quite clearly passing by a series of lakes. What makes a lake a lake – is it its size, or whether it freezes over in winter?

'So these must be the highest lakes in the world, then,' I say to Mark, only half in jest.

'No, these are just temporary bodies of water,' he replies (he can be a really interesting guy sometimes). 'They're formed by the glacier melting.'

'I don't understand.'

'Neither do I.'

What's not in dispute is that the scenery's marvellous. We climb above the lake and pitch our campsite looking across it, down the valley to Baruntse and Chamlang. This is up there on my list of the world's top campsites. When we arrive at midday it's sunny, so for the first time in days I have a chance to wash some clothes. True to form, however, there's not enough sun to dry them before it snows later in the afternoon.

We are now camped beneath the Amphu Labtsa, the high, technical pass that I have heard so much about. The British explorer Eric Shipton crossed it from the other side in 1951, towards the end of his Everest reconnaissance expedition. His aim was to find a way round to the Kangshung Face on the east side of Everest, and link up his explorations in Nepal with those of George Mallory on the Tibet side in 1921. He was accompanied by Edmund Hillary, and they were probably the first westerners to look down into the Hongu Valley. Descending from the pass, they camped beside the shores of a lake – who knows, perhaps in the very spot that we are resting now. Shipton realised that to get to the east side of Everest from Nepal, they would need to cross not only the Amphu Labtsa, but two more glaciated passes to the east. These are West Col and East Col, that guard either side of a vast ice plateau to the south of Baruntse. I would love to explore this area myself one day, but for now the Amphu Labtsa will have to do.

It's cold in the evening. We take dinner with Sarki and the kitchen crew in the cook's tent to enable the porters to occupy the mess tent. Someone – I don't remember if it's Siling or Dawa – suggests a 4am wake-up call tomorrow so that we can set off to cross the Amphu Labtsa pass at five o'clock. I respond with disgust – getting up and getting ready in the dark, when it's freezing cold, is not one of my favourite activities. I'll do it for summit days, but only with good reason. Siling, Dawa and Sarki have a quiet talk among themselves and decide to change it to a 4.30 wake-up and 5.30 start. By the time I head back to my tent they have moved it again to a five o'clock wake-up and six o'clock start. This is much more civilised. Now we'll be waking and packing when it's light – though it will still be icy cold.

DAY 16
THE AMPHU LABTSA

Thursday, 7 May 2009 – Imja Tsho, Sagarmatha National Park,
Nepal

Nobody seems to have much enthusiasm for leaving at the crack of dawn. We are roused with bed tea at 5.30, and I put on my down jacket and start packing my things away, but outside everyone is taking it easy. By the time we get away at seven o'clock, the sun has hit the top end of the valley and I'm able to exchange my down jacket for a fleece.

We climb high above the campsite and the lake before slogging up a scree ridge to the foot of a glacier. Behind us the panorama of Baruntse, Chamlang and the Panch Pokhari becomes even more dramatic, and the glacier in front of us leaps its way up to the Amphu Labtsa in a series of thick ice shelves.

Jimmy Roberts struggled to cross the Amphu Labtsa with his porters in 1953 after his first ascent of Mera Peak. Instead, they scrambled up a gully half a mile to the west, where they descended into the Imja Valley and returned to Tengboche. We also find the pass surprisingly technical. Dawa and one of the porters, Pema, spent much of yesterday afternoon putting up fixed ropes; this saves us time today. At the bottom of the glacier we put on harnesses and crampons, and climb a couple of short vertical ice walls. Then we have a steep scramble up rock with a few icy sections to be wary of. Finally there's a sheer snow slope to negotiate.

Mark Dickson and Siling before the
Amphu Labtsa's ice shelves

The vista that greets us at the top is like nothing I've ever seen before. We're now at 5,850m; behind us we can see the other two parts of the well-known Three Cols route between Baruntse and Chamlang over dramatic 6,000m passes of snow and ice to the foot of Makalu (the three cols being the Amphu Labtsa, West Col and East Col). For three days, we walked up the Hongu Valley with the black rock wall of Lhotse straight ahead of us to the north and Everest poking out behind. These features are now right before us and towering over everything.

Just below this huge rock face, looking absolutely pathetic, is 6,189m Island Peak: the mountain we hope to climb shortly. It's so small nestling in front of Lhotse that we have difficulty noticing it at all. None of these mountains appear to be holding much snow, and we know this will make the ascent more difficult. Mark has climbed Island Peak before and he describes the route to us. The steep snow slope onto the summit ridge looks to be a long and difficult ice wall.

We stop for a few minutes for photos before heading down the other side into the Khumbu region of Nepal. We are now in Everest land. After carefully descending a few metres on loose slate, we reach sloping slabs above a drop of a few thousand feet. We stop and wait for the porters to finish lowering their loads down a cliff ahead. These mountain boys have no fear of heights and happily skip along the precarious slabs with no safety equipment. One of them, Bujung, descends the cliff with his 30kg load carried across his forehead on a head strap, despite Siling's strict instructions to stop and lower it.

As for me, I'm grateful to be able to clip in to a safety rope and sit down, perched on a ledge while I wait for our equipment to be lowered. I try to admire the amazing view in front of me, but it's difficult to ignore the huge drop a few inches beyond my toes. I don't enjoy these few minutes of waiting, which seem to go on for a very long time.

Eventually the operation is completed and Dawa gives the signal for us to proceed. Mark traverses quickly along the slabs ahead of us, but I take it more gingerly – not only looking for a good footstep, but also a firm handhold with every move forward. I'm relieved when I reach the cliff face and can produce my figure-of-eight device to abseil down the rope. I attach myself, lean back and leap down happily, feeling safe for the first time in several minutes. After a short drop I reach a second rope, but I estimate the one I'm attached to is long enough to carry me to safety, so I continue sliding down it.

A moment of comedy follows. I don't realise that my rope is anchored to the rock where the second rope begins, and a few feet below the anchor I start turning upside down. An emergency manoeuvre is called for. I right myself again and climb back up the rock as far as I can, until I reach a smooth section and can climb no further. But one of my feet is still caught the wrong side of a taut rope – I find it difficult to get my leg over (as the bishop said to the actress).

I have no option but to detach my figure-of-eight from the first rope and attach it to the second one – but after clipping in with my safety carabiner and detaching the figure-of-eight, I realise the second rope is a long way away and I'm going to have to free climb across to it. However, at that moment one of the porters waiting at the bottom, Drukchen, realises my predicament. He skips up the ice slope I'm about to abseil down, tosses me the rope, and skips back down again.

I attach my figure-of-eight to the second rope and follow him. My embarrassment increases when I reach a point where I judge it will now be comfortable to walk across. I detach myself from the rope, only to find that the oldest of the porters, Lhakpa, is there to take my arm. He guides me to a wider ledge where all the porters and Mark are waiting. I feel like an old pensioner being led to a rest home. No sooner do I sit down on a slab than two of the other porters start helping me to take my boots and crampons off and change into my walking boots. It's all too much for my brain to cope with, but they're not finished. When I stand up, they start helping me with my harness. At least they don't try taking it off with their teeth like Dawa did the other day.

The ledge below the cliff is a little wider than the one above, but it's still a long way down. Although I'm glad when Siling and Dawa finish packing away the fixed ropes and climb down to join us, my response is terse when Siling suggests this seems like a nice spot for lunch.

We continue down 400m of crappy, slatey, gravelly stuff pockmarked with slippery ice to keep me on my toes. Although the risk of falling down a cliff has gone, the odds of ending up on my backside have increased. In Scotland, it's the sort of slope that causes me to climb down the other side of a hill and walk back round to avoid it. Finally we reach a sandy beach at the bottom of this slate quarry and stop for lunch. Looking back up the rock face we've just descended, it's hard to fathom what gave Shipton (or anyone) the idea this might be a pass, but in reality I've enjoyed it, despite a few hairy moments on this side.

The remainder of the afternoon is straightforward trekking. After wading across the beach through fine sand, we round a hillside and find ourselves passing along a grassy ridge with Island Peak up ahead of us, still dwarfed by Lhotse's giant south face. It's fine walking. We reach camp at the far end of the glacial lake of Imja Tsho at three o'clock, tired but exhilarated.

'Lhakpa is worried about some of the porters in the KE group,' Siling tells us later. They have spent an extra rest day on the other side of the pass and will be coming over tomorrow. 'He says they're not mountain boys, and thinks they will struggle to get over the pass.'

'Hopefully Ade will warn his clients to pack their kit bags carefully tomorrow,' Mark says. 'If they think they're going to be gently lowered over the pass they're in for a surprise. It was more of an uncontrolled hurl over the cliff today.'

Mark's comment proves quite prescient.

At dinner, Mark, Siling and I agree to have a rest day tomorrow. Although carrying our kit up to high camp tomorrow for a 2am summit attempt is within our capabilities, we still have plenty of spare days before we need to catch flights back to Kathmandu. We could all do with a rest after sixteen consecutive days of exertion. We inspected Island Peak thoroughly on our way down and concluded that it's going to be a tricky climb because of the state of the snow – we could do with tackling it in a more refreshed state.

It's a remarkable mountain, a sheer lump of rock sticking up 1,000m from the surrounding terrain. From most angles it looks isolated from all the surrounding peaks. In reality, part of it is attached to Lhotse, and in some ways it can be described as an extension to the south ridge of Lhotse's second summit, Lhotse Shar. The name Island Peak was given to it by members of the 1953 Everest expedition, because it resembled an island rising out of an enormous sea of ice. It was officially renamed Imja Tse in 1983, but most people still use its original name. The 1953 team also climbed Island Peak's south-west summit as a warm up to the main event: the first ascent of Everest. Tenzing Norgay, Charles Evans, Charles Wylie, Alfred Gregory and seven other Sherpas besides Tenzing all climbed it while they tested their brand new open-circuit oxygen apparatus. In his report of the ascent, Wylie said that Tenzing had led for most of the way. He also reported that the tests had been successful. The Sherpas said that oxygen made climbing uphill seem like walking on the flat, though one of them – Ang Temba – went a step further, claiming that it made uphill seem like downhill.

The main summit of Island Peak was first climbed in 1956 by Hans-Rudolf Von Gunten and two unnamed Sherpas. They were members of a Swiss team who went on to make the second ascent of Everest and first ascent of Lhotse. I'm sure it must have been easy for elite climbers such as these. It will be harder for me, but I expect we shall be fine. With very little snow on it, just a few glaciers trickling down from the summit ridge are enough to prevent it from being a rock climb.

DAY 17
DUST STORM

Friday, 8 May 2009 – Imja Tsho, Sagarmatha National Park, Nepal

We take full advantage of our rest day by lazing around camp, but we're not always comfortable. Our tents are pitched in a dusty cove a few feet above the icy glacial river of Imja Khola, and we enjoy a pleasant breakfast sitting outside and admiring clear skies over Lhotse and Island Peak. At first it's difficult to move from this comfy spot; Mark and I recline in our seats and drink copious quantities of tea.

At nine o'clock the wind starts picking up. The combination of sun and wind make for a good drying day, so I go down to the river to wash some clothes. I hang them out on a washing line fixed between the two smaller tents and retire inside for a lie down. By lunchtime I'm annoyed to discover that the wind has whipped up the surface dust and coated my washing in a fine silvery sand. Now it looks like I have a set of silver-sequined underpants.

Imja Tsho camp, with views of Lhotse and Island Peak

In the afternoon Mark and I are caught between a rock and a hard place. Outside a dust storm rages, but inside the tent it's sweltering; we can't allow ourselves too much ventilation because open tent flaps allow the silvery sand to blow into the tent and cover everything inside. It reaches 40ºC inside. We opt for sweltering heat as we sit with our shirts off, preferring a film of sweat to a film of dust. Still, it's good to be lazy for a change.

Then, to prove there's no logic to the weather, later in the afternoon it snows. All the porters huddle into the mess tent for warmth and shelter as we have afternoon tea.

At 5.30 two clients from the KE group turn up at our campsite asking if we know where theirs is. They are just the vanguard, having set off at six o'clock this morning; as Lhakpa and Mark predicted, they've not had an easy day. Two kit bags came loose as they were being lowered down this side of the pass, and fell hundreds of metres down to the bottom. They managed to recover most of the contents, but much of it was shredded, including Therm-a-Rests and sleeping bags. They're going to be tired and depressed when they get into camp tonight. We wonder how many of them will be following us to high camp on Island Peak tomorrow.

DAY 18
LHOTSE

Saturday, 9 May 2009 – Island Peak, Sagarmatha National Park, Nepal

We make a leisurely start from camp this morning. Sarki tells us it will only take three and a half hours to get to Island Peak high camp from here, but we complete the journey in a little over two. Pasang the assistant cook will be remaining in this dusty cove to look after most of our kit while we attempt Island Peak. We're taking only our essentials up to high camp.

This morning's short walk is amazing. Within ten minutes of leaving camp at 8.30 we find ourselves walking beneath the enormous south face of Lhotse. We're already at 5,000m, but it towers 3½km above us in a single sheer wall of rock and ice – the scale is hard to comprehend. The top third is so steep and windblown that it's holding hardly any snow – it's just a jagged wall of black rock. The bottom two thirds hold a colossal mass of snow in tiers of hanging seracs and fragile powder. There are frequent rumbles like thunder as avalanches tumble down its flanks every few minutes.

It's hard to believe anyone would ever consider climbing such an obvious death trap, but elite climbers have a different mentality to normal folk, and for some of them the risk of death is considered a plus point. Lhotse was first climbed from the Western Cwm on the opposite side by the Swiss climbers Fritz Luchsinger and Ernst Reiss in 1956 – during the same expedition that Von Gunten climbed Island Peak. It wasn't until 1973 that anyone was tempted to have a go at the south face. A Japanese team made an attempt that year, and for nearly twenty years the south face of Lhotse became one of the holy grails of Himalayan mountaineering. It thwarted such illustrious names as Reinhold Messner and Ricardo Cassin. Most were driven back by the grave avalanche risk. Then in 1989, the great Polish mountaineer Jerzy Kukuczka climbed most of the way up, and was just 200m below the summit when a rope snapped. He fell 3,000m to his death. His shocked climbing partner Ryszard Pawlowski abandoned the attempt, and somehow climbed down safely on his own.

It wasn't until 1990 that anyone succeeded, and that was in controversial circumstances. The Slovenian Tomo Česen claimed a solo ascent of the face that had defeated better known climbers for years. There were no witnesses and no summit photos, and many people doubt whether he actually succeeded. A few months later a strong Russian team did succeed using siege tactics, but they also expressed disbelief about Česen's climb.

I don't know whether to admire these people or not. Of course, they are all amazing climbers and incredibly brave. The south face of Lhotse is awesome, but as I look up at its towering presence, I can't help thinking that they must be crazy.

We skirt the south side of Island Peak, with Baruntse and its outlying ridges up ahead of us, and climb the steep zigzag path up Island Peak's south flank to high camp at a little under 5,500m. Although we're in the high glacial regions, birdlife is everywhere – I stop frequently to film snow cocks (known locally as *kongma*), accentors and rose finches.

The climb to high camp is a little strange at times. Looking straight up at Island Peak's summit ridge, there are moments when gargantuan Lhotse appears behind it. Lhotse stands at 8,516m, which means its summit is battered by the jet-stream winds that circle the Earth above 8,000m. Plumes of spindrift hare off its top – but from our position it looks like they are coming off Island Peak. Thankfully, the winds on Island Peak's summit are not so murderous (or so we hope).

High camp is comfortable, although Gombu and Karma have to climb for forty minutes above our tents to the start of the glacier to get ice to melt for water. A Jagged Globe group on its way down from the summit passes through camp at midday. After that we have the place to ourselves for a couple of hours. It's so peaceful.

Although the KE group turns up at two o'clock, I was expecting the place to be busier. I spend the afternoon in my tent reading my Everest trekking guide, trying to plan the extra nine or ten days I'll have to myself, trekking around the Khumbu region after we've climbed Island Peak. We eat Sherpa stew in the cook's tent at 5.30; after that we try to get as much sleep as we can before our middle-of-the-night start for Island Peak's summit.

DAY 19
KNIFE-EDGE RIDGE

Sunday, 10 May 2009 – Island Peak, Sagarmatha National Park, Nepal

I sleep with my ear plugs in to avoid being woken up even earlier than planned by the sound of cooks getting up in the middle of the night to prepare breakfast. I don't hear Gombu's traditional greeting of, 'Good morning, sir,' outside the tent at 2.45am – something that has become one of the joys of the trek. Instead, Mark bashes me crudely awake with a punch.

I swing into action straight away, putting on all the kit I prepared last night: two pairs of trousers, base layer, fleece, down jacket, and all the rest. But then I pause and stop acting on automatic. It feels incredibly warm inside the tent, and although the temperature is well below freezing, it must be the mildest conditions I've ever experienced prior to a 6,000m-peak summit day. I decide to ditch my fleece and put it in my pack instead.

At three o'clock the KE group set off for their summit climb. The rest of our team huddle inside the cook's tent. Last night I told them not to cook me too much for breakfast, as I'm rarely able to eat in the middle of the night unless it's a doner kebab and I've just come back from a night on the booze. I manage an omelette and copious quantities of tea. Hydration is usually a good idea, though it may also prove to be a mistake: I'll be wearing a harness for the next few hours, and it won't be easy going for a pee.

We set off at 3.30am with Dawa leading, followed by Mark, myself, and Siling. Behind us Karma carries a bag with our mountaineering boots and crampons. The first 350m of the climb is on rock, and although we're sacrificing some of the warmth of triple-layered plastic boots, it's sure as hell easier walking up the rocky path in ordinary walking boots. On the down side, the toe of my left boot is still being held together with gaffer tape.

The path leads up a gully and onto a grey rock ridge. Somehow Dawa manages to find his way in the dark as the trail weaves up and around boulders, but the Sherpa leading KE's group is not finding it quite so easy. The head torches of their group bob up and down above us at first, but all of a sudden we find ourselves level with them, and their Sherpa shouts across to Dawa to say that he's lost the path. We're glad to be ahead of them now – they're a slow group and opportunities to overtake might be scarce higher up the mountain.

By 4.45 we've crossed the rock section and arrive at

a glacier. We've already completed half the vertical ascent, but that was the easy bit. It's now light enough to switch off our head torches. Karma unpacks the bag and we put on our plastic boots and crampons. It still feels very warm for a summit day, and I remove my down mitts in favour of the superior manual dexterity of ordinary gloves.

Before long the four of us are roped together and Dawa is leading us onto the glacier. The path weaves through undulating ice and reaches a large, deep, forked crevasse where somebody has put two aluminium ladders across the gap. Thankfully they're so short that I only need to step on one rung in my cramponned feet before making a long stride to the other side – no need to look down into the yawning abyss beneath my feet. After this we cross a wide glaciated plateau on our way to the daunting headwall leading onto the summit ridge.

The plateau steepens the nearer we approach the headwall. Dawa seems to be on a mission to reach the summit as quickly as possible. I struggle to keep up with his pace; instead of building up a rhythm and plodding behind him slowly like I did on Mera, this time I have to keep asking him to stop every few paces so that I can get my breath back. Even when we stop, I can feel the tug on the rope as he longs to keep moving.

Then we reach the headwall, over 100m of steep ice. When Mark climbed Island Peak in 2005, he said there was a lot more snow on the mountain, much of it glazing the headwall, making it an easier climb.

Now there is no snow at all on the surface, and we have to make our way up rock-hard ice steps, often a metre or two high. Somebody has put a fixed line up the headwall onto the summit ridge. This assists somewhat; I clip into the rope with my jumar and haul myself up, but still there is a lot of front-pointing with my crampons and some very big steps, which I find exhausting. As an additional precaution in case the fixed rope is unsafe, Dawa keeps us roped together. This means we have to remain a short distance apart – not always easy when we're having to scramble up two or three metres at a time before taking a rest.

When I finally scramble onto the ridge and find myself staring at the massive south face of Lhotse I give a surprised cheer. The final few metres to the summit are comparatively easy but extremely dramatic. It's a steep climb along a knife-edge crest, with a wide view across to Baruntse on the right, completely dwarfed by Lhotse on the left. When I look back down the ridge to Mark and Siling behind me on the rope, the view is no less breathtaking. We joined the ridge close to the summit, but it extends much further back, embracing the full length of the mountain in a narrow blade of rock and ice, with Ama Dablam rising up in an elegant arch of ice behind. At the end of this ridge is the south-west summit, first climbed by Tenzing Norgay and his party. It looked a similar height to the main summit as we approached from the Amphu Labtsa, but now it's clearly lower.

*Mark Dickson approaches the summit of Island Peak, with
Ama Dablam on the near horizon behind*

The ridge steepens and we step onto the summit at eight o'clock. Although it's big enough to accommodate a few people, it drops away precipitously on all sides, and we remain clipped into the fixed line while we take our summit pictures and videos. For once Everest hides behind Lhotse, but our view of the latter is about as close as you can get without actually climbing the thing.

Plenty of other 8,000m peaks are visible. The symmetrical black pyramid of Makalu sits behind a col ahead of us, and the wider, convoluted white wall of Cho Oyu forms the horizon to the left of the Lhotse-Nuptse ridge. Then Dawa points out a big mountain on the far horizon, well beyond Cho Oyu: Shishapangma. It's the first time that I've seen this isolated mountain in Tibet.

We have the summit to ourselves for our half-hour stay, but Island Peak's summit ridge is not a place to be caught too late in the morning when the winds begin to pick up. We pass the first climbers from the KE party a little further down the ridge. If I thought we were going to have a quick and easy descent, I'm sorely mistaken.

The fixed line up the headwall is strung out with climbers from top to bottom, so we need to go a little further along and leave the ridge at a different point. One by one we have to abseil down not one but two rope lengths, which involves a lot of waiting around at both the tops and bottoms of each pitch. There is a third pitch before we reach the plateau, but by now the gradient of the headwall has lessened sufficiently for us to descend roped together.

Crossing the glacier, we look back and see dozens of little black dots on their way up the headwall and summit ridge. We were fortunate to reach the summit first, as we had on Mera, and avoided the inevitable traffic jams. The summit is becoming more dangerous now the morning is wearing on. We leave the glacier and look back as we're putting our walking boots back on to see little figures sitting down in the snow just below the summit, presumably to shelter from the wind. The summit looks to be taking a battering: a huge plume of cloud appears to shoot off it, indicating very high winds, perhaps 150 km/h or more. But this is deceptive. From where we stand Lhotse is hidden directly behind the summit of Island

Peak, and in reality these winds are almost certainly striking Lhotse, 2½km higher up in the Earth's atmosphere, rather than Island Peak.

We quickly descend the rock band and are back in our tents at high camp at 11.30, eight hours after starting out. It has taken us nearly as long to descend as ascend. Gombu brings tea and noodles to our tent, but I still don't feel like eating. We pack away as quickly as we can.

Three of our porters – the youngsters Drukchen, Tashi and Pemba – have come up to high camp to carry our things, and they are as keen to get going as we are. Everyone else has packed and gone. The only tent remaining at high camp belongs to KE's cook.

'What's that smell?' I ask Dawa. 'Can you smell it?'

He looks confused. 'Smell, what smell?'

'You can't smell it? I can smell it, and so can Mark. It's the smell of Everest beer.'

Everybody laughs. We've not had a beer since we left Kathmandu.

Dawa puts on his pack and leads the way down the mountain. It's 12.30, and the weather is starting to worsen, spurring us to move quickly. A gale is blasting in our faces as we cross the sandy valley south of Island Peak; although I'm only wearing my Icebreaker top, rather than stopping to layer up it seems simpler just to walk faster to reach the shelter of Chukhung as soon as possible. This certainly seems to be Mark and Dawa's strategy, and I find myself chasing their backs a few hundred metres in front of me most of the way down. We reach our windy campsite after only an hour. Here I finally put on my fleece when it starts to snow. But this only puts me further behind Mark and Dawa, and makes me all the more determined to keep up with them. Meanwhile Siling casually strolls along at my pace, stopping to wait for me when necessary.

The unpleasant cold, windy and overcast conditions continue all the way to Chukhung. At 4,700m, it's the first outpost of civilisation below the high glacial regions where we've spent the last week, ever since we were in Khare before climbing Mera Peak. We reach the village at 2.30, cold and tired, and when Gombu brings hot tea, the beers are quickly forgotten.

This is the last day of our expedition. While I now have ten days to explore the Khumbu region on foot with my backpack, everyone else is keen to get home. It's the last time we're going to be together, so Mark and I decide to buy *chang*, the local rice beer, for all the crew. A large bowl of milky fluid appears. It may look like milk, but it's a good deal more potent.

An evening of mayhem, singing and dancing follows, led by the old chap, Lhakpa, who keeps trying to drag everyone onto the 'dance floor' however reluctant they may be (I use inverted commas for good reason). Most comical is Sarki, who happens to be carrying a kettle when Lhakpa collars him, and tries his best to wriggle free without much success. I manage to capture some of his hilarious kettle dance on video.

By comparison Mark and I have a sober evening.

The *chang* is made from local water that probably hasn't been boiled. Our delicate western stomachs are likely to find it unpalatable, and I don't want to spend the next few days hovering over the toilet and bunging myself up with Imodium to enable safe passage from village to village. We confine our celebrations to two small tins of San Miguel beer each.

Meanwhile Siling is more concerned about the KE group. Shortly after we arrived in Chukhung it started snowing heavily, and as the sun goes down and day turns to night the snow continues to fall. Other than the three quick ones who are safely in camp and wondering what's happened to their companions, there's no sign of them. Some head torches are just appearing over the hillside when I decide to call it a night at 8pm.

DAY 20
MONKS AND SNOW STORMS

Monday, 11 May 2009 – Pangboche, Sagarmatha
National Park, Nepal

Despite the copious quantities of *chang* they drunk last night, our crew seem surprisingly lively this morning. A knock on the door shortly before seven o'clock signals the last of Gombu's black tea wake-up calls. I have quite a bit of packing to do – I need to strip my kit down to the essentials for the next ten days now that the porters are leaving us and I'll be carrying all my own kit. Fortunately, the profusion of teahouses in the Everest region means that there's plenty of accommodation and good food to be found every day.

I had an ambitious programme for my ten days – including two high passes and several well-known viewpoints – but looking outside this morning I've decided to slim it down. It's still snowing heavily and low-lying cloud banks the landscape. Although I can't do anything about the weather and views, I realise that relying on being able to cross a high pass on a certain day may mess up my itinerary if there continues to be a great deal of snow. I had intended to head up to Gorak Shep and Kala Patthar today, and then go to Gokyo after visiting Everest Base Camp. But this would have meant crossing a high pass called the Cho La. I decide that it's safer to head straight to Gokyo along the valley. I have a feeling deep in my bones that I'll be hitting the Everest Base Camp trail again some day, but a thorough exploration of the Gokyo Lakes region is less likely. I still have a few days to play with, but now I can take it easier and leave less to chance – though I'll still need luck with the weather.

After giving our porters and kitchen crew a send-off, Dawa, Siling, Mark and I leave Chukhung at 8.45. As we're leaving, Ade catches our attention from the KE campsite. We stop to hear his story. Although he succeeded in getting all of his clients to the top of Island Peak, when they came to descend, two of them didn't want to abseil – they had never done it before – so he had to lower them instead. Snow was lying thick on the ground by the time they slogged back through high camp at 4.30pm. He was the last to arrive in Chukhung shortly before 9pm, and the last two or three hours were in the dark. Thankfully they were all carrying head torches from their 3am start that morning. An eighteen-hour day on lowly Island Peak – Ade and his team must be shattered.

It continues to snow heavily as we descend from Chukhung. Passing through the first village of

Dingboche is a depressing scene, with atrocious visibility in thick snow. This is where I intended to leave the others and head north, but right now I'm not regretting my decision to limit my ambitions. We continue onward. By the time we reach Pangboche the snow has ceased and the sun is trying to peep through. I catch glimpses of the trail as the path passes high above the river, and once or twice the mountains of Kangtega and Thamserku reveal themselves through the cloud.

We stop for lunch at the Highland Sherpa Lodge in Pangboche. Here I say my goodbyes to Mark, Siling and Dawa, who leave at one o'clock for Namche and their flight out of Lukla tomorrow. I'm starting to feel more hopeful about the weather, but it's still not clear enough for me to be tempted by a walk around the village and up to the monastery in the mist high above. I unpack my things and hang them up to dry in my room before retiring to spend the afternoon in the warm dining area.

At about four o'clock, a dozen monks from the monastery invade the peace. They arrive dressed in a motley assortment of robes, down jackets and cowboy hats, and they've brought drums, cymbals and red squeaky clarinets. I'm guessing there are no music teachers in Pangboche, for they spend an hour or more chanting and raising a cacophony while the lady lodge owner whizzes around, filling their glasses with milk tea and a milky fluid I now recognise as *chang*. Several hangers-on arrive with them, ranging in age from small boys to wizened old men, and at the end of the first chanting session they toss rice into the air. The landlady is insistent the monks accept all the drinks she offers them, and gets quite upset when any of them decline. As they are leaving, she catches the oldest by the shoulder of his robe, drags him back into the room, and forces him to down a whole glass of *chang* – which he gamely does before she lets him leave.

The snow has returned by the time the fun is over. By early evening, it's covering everything in a thick carpet, and its accompanying mist lies damply over the village. If it continues like this all night, I may need to revise my plans for a second time.

DAY 21
INTO THE GOKYO VALLEY

Tuesday, 12 May 2009 – Dole, Sagarmatha National Park,
Nepal

I've arranged breakfast for seven o'clock this morning, hoping that the skies are clear and I can make an early start towards Gokyo. Siling warned me that avalanches can threaten the high trail from Pangboche to Phortse (the direct route into the Gokyo Valley from here). The alternative – already my third choice of access into the Gokyo Valley – involves walking to the village of Kjanjuma, most of the way back to Namche, to access the valley from the western side. That's a long diversion and I'm hoping I don't have to resort to it.

When I get up at 6.30 to go outside for a pee, the carpet of snow has grown to several inches and it's continuing to fall. Upstairs in the warm and comfortable restaurant area, some of the guests are already making plans to stay another day. Two Canadian parties – one a group of female medics and the other a young family – are going nowhere. There are two other couples in the lodge, both of whom are also heading to Gokyo. The helpful lady lodge owner convinces all of us that the trail to Phortse is safe albeit precarious. One couple set off at eight while it's still snowing heavily, but I'm more cautious.

Content to bide my time, I pack all my things in preparation for departure, order a pot of black tea, and sit in the warmth of the lodge. Sure enough, it stops snowing shortly before ten o'clock. The sun burns a hole in the cloud and reveals the trail high above me. Needing no further invitation, I pay my bill, say my goodbyes and leave.

A steep climb above the lodge brings me up to the main Phortse trail at Pangboche Monastery. I'm able to follow a single set of footprints through the snow. Once on the main trail things are easier, as plenty of people have been past this morning, and for about an hour the walking is fantastic: the sky is clear and the landscape sparkles under heavy drapes of snow, a winter wonderland. Behind me the shapely peak of Ama Dablam rises high with its oval summit and armchair shoulders stretched out on either side. Far down the valley in front I see the red crown of Tengboche Monastery, a place I visited seven years ago, perched high on a ridge on the other side of the valley. The trail snakes along the hillside high above the Imja Khola River, which I've followed all the way from Island Peak. The walking is exhilarating.

But soon a cold mist rolls in from further down the valley and the views are over. The snow is beginning to melt and I spend much of the section between Pangboche and Phortse wading through a sludge of molten slush, up and down slippery rock steps carved in the hillside. When I round a corner and see the village below me, I lose my way skirting around it. I need to find a path down to the river, but it's not easy to find underneath all the fresh snow. Eventually I meet a man on a horse who leads me around the edge of the village at a fast trot and points out the trail down into rhododendron woods. I descend steeply all the way to the river, cross over a bridge and start up the other side.

I pass the afternoon with a steep climb through more rhododendron forest as I head north along the Dudh Kosi Valley towards Gokyo. The path has now become a quagmire of mud. Without doubt it's the muddiest day of the trek so far. I reach the village of Dole at 2.45 and move into the first teahouse I find, the Namaste Lodge. It's basic, but small and cosy. Everybody else who arrives behind me seems to be checking into the larger Alpine Cottage Lodge just below it. At four o'clock I'm joined by a mixed-nationality party of three: an Australian, another Canadian, and a Thai girl. Someone fires up the stove in the cosy dining area. Then, depressingly, it starts snowing again.

DAY 22
ARRIVAL IN GOKYO

Wednesday, 13 May 2009 – Gokyo, Sagarmatha National Park, Nepal

When I look out of my bedroom window at 6.15 this morning, I see blue sky. I'm keeping my fingers crossed the heavy snow of the last three days has finally come to an end.

I arranged my breakfast for seven o'clock. I eat my fried eggs – which look suspiciously like an omelette – pay up, and leave Dole shortly after 7.30. I seem to be the only person making such an early start; until I reach the village of Machermo two hours later, I see nobody else on the trail. Unfortunately, I soon realise my hopes for better weather are doomed. Blue sky teases me for about an hour, and I'm briefly able to see the summit of Kangtega when I look back down the valley towards Phortse. But the clouds quickly close in and I see no views for the rest of the day.

Machermo was the scene of a famous yeti encounter, related by the travel writer Bruce Chatwin in his essay *On Yeti Tracks*. Chatwin described meeting a Sherpani (female Sherpa) called Lakpa Doma in the village of Khumjung while he was trekking in the Khumbu region. Through an interpreter she described how she was tending the family yaks in a field near Machermo in 1974, when a yeti jumped out from behind a rock and dragged her over to a stream. She knew it was a yeti because it had yellow eyes, big ridges above its eyebrows, and hollow temples. It proceeded to slaughter three of the yaks by twisting their horns. When some policemen came up from Namche to examine the crime scene, they agreed that the yaks could not have been killed by a man.

I walk nervously through the village, hoping I don't have to dump my rucksack and make a run for it. Luckily, there are no yetis today.

A blanket of snow covers the trail beyond Machermo. The path climbs steadily towards Gokyo, climaxing in a steep rock staircase hewn into a cliff. After this, it flattens out abruptly and I find myself passing the first of Gokyo's lakes, Longponga – really nothing more than a small tarn. It's strange how places can look more civilised on a map. Emerging onto a cold snowy trail surrounded by mist and black cliffs, it's hard to imagine a bleaker scene than this, but I'm amazed to see a solitary shelduck floating across the black water of the lake.

The snow continues as I pass through a monochrome valley with peaks and lakes to my left, and the steep lateral moraine of the Ngozumba Glacier to my right. Tired but relieved, I reach Gokyo at one o'clock: a settlement of trekkers' lodges on the shores of Dudh Pokhari, the Third Lake, and walled in behind by the high moraine of the Ngozumba Glacier. I check in to another place called the Namaste Lodge, which both Siling and two French trekkers I met on the way up recommended to me. It has a fine location overlooking the lake, and a comfortable upstairs dining room with a central fireplace and plenty of sunlight spilling through three walls of windows. Four other people share the lodge with me today: a young German couple who were in the lodge at Pangboche, and a South African/English couple called Ren and Phil (who, it emerges, are not a couple at all, but just friends).

As the afternoon turns to evening, for once it doesn't snow and the skies seem to be clearing. I take a chance on ordering a 5.30am breakfast tomorrow in the hope it's a beautiful day and I can climb Gokyo Ri, a popular Everest viewpoint above the village, and actually see something.

Here at 4,800m altitude it's still cold in the evening, and the staff at the Namaste Lodge are having stove difficulties. Every time they stoke it up with more fuel, it smokes like crazy; they have to open two or three windows to let a draught in, negating any benefit from having it in the first place. Apart from this the lodge is excellent. Because I've arrived after the main trekking season is considered to have finished, my room is provided free of charge – as long as I don't go anywhere else to eat.

DAY 23
THE PERFECT GOKYO RI EXPERIENCE

Thursday, 14 May 2009 – Gokyo, Sagarmatha National Park,
Nepal

I can hardly believe my luck to discover that after four days of snow, the skies are clear this morning. I'm overjoyed, and so glad I pushed through to Gokyo in the bad weather yesterday to wake up to this.

After a tasty breakfast of fried egg and toast, I set off up Gokyo Ri at 5.45am. My guidebook gives the less-than-helpful estimate of one and a half to three hours to reach the top. From the lodge the summit looks in touching distance and little more than an hour's climb away, but distances can be deceptive in the Himalayas. The total ascent from Gokyo is around 550m – I'd have to be tonning it to reach the top in an hour.

After only 100m of climbing, I hit snow. It's hard compacted stuff that makes for tiring work, and it gets thicker the higher I get. There is far more of it than there looked from the bottom; I reach the summit at 7.45 after two hours of hard slog.

But it's well worth it. The summit is a maze of cairns and prayer flags covering a wide area, and it takes me a couple of guesses before I find the highest point. The view is something else. Right below me to the east is the vast Ngozumba Glacier, the largest in Nepal, blanketing the ground immediately beneath Gokyo Ri in a long white and brown ribbon. On the opposite side of the glacier, and spanning its length from top to bottom, is a tangle of icy ridges and towering snow peaks stretching to the far horizon.

I have been among high mountains many times, but this is like nowhere I have ever seen. Cho Oyu is by far the most prominent at the head of the glacier, little more than the clang of a yak bell away; then Gyachung Kang, Chakung, Cholo, Changtse, Everest, Lhotse, Nirekha, Makalu, Lobuje, Cholatse and Taboche follow in sequence, with Kangtega and Thamserku completing the eastern panorama at the bottom end of the valley. Four of the peaks are among the six highest on Earth, with Everest and Lhotse crowning the eastern horizon like watchtowers. Some, like Cholatse, which rises across the glacier from Third Lake like a giant teepee, look truly terrifying. This mountain has been classified as a trekking peak, like Mera and Island, but the only way you'd be able to trek this one is by turning it on its side.

On the western side, looking over the Renjo La pass, I see a less familiar horizon of peaks in the Rolwaling region of Nepal. I hope to cross the pass and leave the Gokyo Valley if conditions are favourable. Immediately below me, Gokyo nestles on the banks of Dudh Pokhari, the Third Lake. The Second Lake, Taboche Tsho, peeks over a shoulder of hillside behind it. High above me to the south, rising from the shores of the Third Lake, is the jagged crest of Phari Lapche. I witness a huge avalanche tumbling down its face, throwing up a cloud of powder snow worryingly close to the Renjo La trail.

Mark Horrell on the summit of Gokyo Ri (5,360m)
with Everest and Lhotse behind

I spend an hour and a half, spellbound, surrounded by the summit snows. All of the mountains are remarkable, but Cho Oyu dominates, a wall of snow at the top end of the valley. It is considered to be the easiest 8,000m peak to climb, but not from this side. First climbed from the Tibet side in

1954 by Pasang Dawa Lama and the Austrians Herbert Tichy and Sepp Jöchler, it wasn't until Reinhold Messner climbed the south-west flank with Hans Kammerlander and Michl Dacher in 1983 that there was an ascent from this side. They climbed the peak in alpine style with three overnight bivouacs.

Gokyo Ri is normally a big tourist peak with hordes of people climbing it every day, but I'm entirely alone except for an alpine accentor springing from rock to rock nearby, hoping I leave it some food. I have the place to myself for all that time. It's a perfect experience. Only when I leave the summit at 9.30 do I pass the young German couple coming up.

Back at the Namaste Lodge I have tea and noodle soup before heading above Gokyo onto the lateral moraine of the Ngozumba Glacier. I walk along the crest of the moraine as far as the Fourth Lake. The skies are starting to cloud over, hiding some of the peaks, but there's no hiding the vast glacier below me, dirty with moraine and spattered with little grey lakes of molten ice. I hear it creaking; every so often a piece of moraine breaks off and crashes a hundred feet or more down to the glacier. I keep a few feet away from the edge to avoid going with it.

Yesterday there was just a hard core of us prepared to push through to Gokyo in the snow, but now the weather has improved everyone seems to be coming. The Namaste Lodge was very quiet last night with only five of us staying here. Tonight, it's packed with trekkers who have mainly arrived in pairs.

DAY 24
NGOZUMBA TSHO, THE FIFTH LAKE

Friday, 15 May 2009 – Gokyo, Sagarmatha National Park,
Nepal

I make another early start, this time to head further
north into the Gokyo Valley and reach the Fifth Lake.
There's a slight delay while Richard, my companion
for the day, waits for boiled eggs to put in his packed
lunch. I met the 29-year-old from Nottingham in the
lodge yesterday afternoon; he has quit his job to travel
around the world for a year. He's already been in the
Annapurnas prior to this, so he's well acclimatised,
but otherwise this is his first experience of trekking.
He's inquisitive and asks me lots of questions. He
turns out to be an amiable companion for the day, and
hopefully the feeling is mutual. He tells me later that
he would have walked right past Everest without
realising it was there had I not pointed it out to him.

We set off at 6.15. For most of the first three hours
the views are clear and stunning. Cho Oyu rises up
ahead as the path weaves between hillsides on the left

and the moraine of the Ngozumba Glacier on the right. Shortly before we reach the Fifth Lake, we get our first views of Everest peeping out over the crest of the moraine. At the Fifth Lake, Ngozumba Tsho, the path fizzles out and we scramble across rocks to the far corner, where we're surprised to see a small campsite of three sleeping tents and a large mess tent. It's now 9.15; we discuss whether to continue beyond it to the Sixth Lake, or climb a hillside above the Fifth Lake to a viewpoint that Siling recommended to me, where unusual views of Everest can be seen.

We opt for the latter, and initially the decision is vindicated. As we rise above the moraine and look out along the full length of the Ngozumba Glacier, we can see a fresh perspective on Everest and Lhotse behind it, with the South Col clearly visible between the two mountains. But before long, the sky clouds over and we don't see Everest again for the rest of the day.

The ascent becomes trickier as we reach deeper snow. We can no longer see the path and have to follow a single set of footprints belonging to someone who has come this way before us – someone who, for all we know, could be as clueless about the route as we are.

Below the summit we have to scramble over boulders for some distance, hazardous in the snow because we can't see where we're putting our feet. It would be easy to stick a leg down a hole and break an ankle, and evacuation from here would not be easy. We reach a surprisingly narrow, rocky summit at

11.15. I measure the altitude on my GPS. We're at 5,520m. Siling was right about the view: when the sky is clear it would offer a unique perspective on Everest, but sadly it has taken us so long to get up here, five hours from Gokyo, that cloud now obscures the peaks. We're within a raven's squawk of Cho Oyu here, but its summit flits in and out of cloud. But leaving aside the hidden mountaintops, the view down the huge Ngozumba Glacier is impressive: a highway of scree-dusted ice spanning the length and breadth of the Gokyo Valley.

*Looking south across the Ngozumba Glacier,
with Fifth Lake below*

We make a circumspect descent, and somehow get down without twisting an ankle or falling on our backsides. Richard suggests asking the people camped by the lake for a cup of tea, but when we're resting at the bottom of the hill eating chocolate, a big bear of a man comes out of one of the tents and starts beating his chest. He lets out a roar and makes a number of other strange noises. I don't know if he has seen us.

'Maybe we won't ask him for a cup of tea,' I say.

'Yeah, perhaps not.'

It takes us two more hours to return to Gokyo, and we arrive at three o'clock. By now it's cold and windy. The sunny weather of the last couple of days will have cleared the passes of snow, but I'm worried there will be fresh snowfall tonight that will put us back to square one.

It's a few hours before Richard appears in the dining room tonight. He is exhausted from our climb. Ren considers our partnership a mismatch, and thinks it's funny that I took him to climb a peak up the valley. Richard is a first-time trekker, and she knows that I will be trying to climb 8,000m Gasherbrum in Pakistan later this year. She wonders how we bonded.

'He was fine,' I tell her. 'It was more of an expedition than we expected, but he didn't complain. He kept up with the pace and just got on with it.'

Ren is also discovering the Khumbu to be a small place, where you often find yourself bumping into people you met several days ago. As she eats dinner, she thinks she recognises an Australian called Scott and a Russian called Ivan, sitting across the dining room from her. She whips out her camera and scans through the photos she's taken – and there they are, right at the beginning. While she and Phil were in Kathmandu waiting to board the bus to Jiri, two crazy westerners jumped onto the roof of a vehicle already crowded with Nepalis just as it was pulling away from the bus station. An accident seemed certain, especially with all the low-slung overhead power cables forcing passengers on the roof to duck. But somehow the accident must have been avoided, because here, nearly three weeks later, are the same two madmen eating *dal bhat* in a lodge high up in the mountains.

DAY 25
ACROSS THE RENJO LA

Saturday, 16 May 2009 – Lungde, Sagarmatha National Park, Nepal

Once again, the weather this morning sparks a swift change of plan. Yesterday afternoon I decided I would go all the way up to Sixth Lake today, repeating three hours of yesterday's trek, but the weather is damp and misty when I arrive at breakfast at 5.30 this morning – I don't fancy walking for three hours to see nothing more than I saw yesterday. The alternative is to press on back to Namche Bazaar and Lukla by heading over the Renjo La pass to the west. Richard is also sitting at breakfast revising his plans, unsure whether to cross over the Cho La to the east in the present conditions. We both decide to wait a little longer and observe the weather.

I head back to my sleeping bag and read another chapter of my book, but very quickly things look more promising. Patches of blue sky appear above the mist as I hurriedly pack my kit and head back to the dining room. The crazy guys Scott and Ivan, and a small organised group with the trekking company Adventure Consultants, are also preparing to cross the Renjo La. While I wait to pay my bill, I talk to a French couple called Ruben and Claire who have taken four months off work. After Nepal, they intend to go climbing in Thailand and Madagascar. Most of the people I meet here seem to be on career breaks or have simply quit their jobs to go travelling.

By 7.15 I'm away, about ten minutes behind Scott and Ivan. As I'm leaving I bump into the Canadian and the Thai girl I met at the lodge in Dole, exploring the shores of Dudh Pokhari. The Thai girl proudly shows me her photos from the previous day.

'Look, we got married yesterday.'

Sure enough, there she is beside the lake in a white wedding dress, which she must have carried all the way up here. I naïvely ask how on Earth they managed to find a priest in Gokyo to carry out the ceremony. The Canadian patiently explains, without a hint of a smile, that there are no priests in Gokyo and the wedding was purely symbolic.

The path up to the Renjo La starts along the edge of Dudh Pokhari. Soon afterwards, it begins climbing a grassy hillside through patches of dwarf rhododendron that I'm surprised to see growing at this altitude. The view behind me, across the lake to Gokyo, is picturesque. I soon forget about it as I begin climbing, first up a rocky pathway, then following footprints in the snow to reach a broad plateau. From now on, it's a slog through snow as I follow step by step in someone else's footprints. I cross the plateau then plod up rocky banks in thick snow.

I reach the pass shortly after ten o'clock. The clouds have closed in and it feels bleak. Pausing only for a quick photo underneath the prayer flags with my back to Gokyo, I descend on the other side, following the two black figures of Scott and Ivan on the trail below me. The snow is deeper here, but a clearer path zigzags down to a small black lake. Here I put my pack down for my first rest since leaving Gokyo. Despite the snow, I've managed to plod over the pass without stopping, and I'm not feeling exhausted like I expected.

The remainder of the walk is much more pleasant, across green moorland, past two more lakes with wide sandy beaches, and along a path cut into a hillside above a wide hanging valley. I reach the village of Lungde at one o'clock and decide to stop for the night at the Renjo Pass Support Lodge. Ivan is there already, but he's lost his friend Scott, who descended all the way to the Bhote Khosi River, which spills down from the Nangpa La pass and the Tibetan border to our north.

Lungde sits a few hundred metres above the valley, and Scott won't be able to see the village from the river, so Ivan is doubtful whether he will be able to find us. A little while later, the Adventure Consultants group arrives. Their leader asks us to share a room so that they can have their own private dormitory. Ivan and I happily agree – though it means that if Scott turns up I'll have to move again.

Somehow I don't feel surprised by this turn of events. To me, Scott seemed a carefree soul, while Ivan was the quiet, sensible one in the partnership. When they first showed up at the Namaste Lodge in Gokyo, Scott asked me how long it took to climb Gokyo Ri. A few minutes later I looked out of the window and saw the pair of them on their way up. Ivan had a rucksack and a pair of walking poles, but Scott was carrying absolutely nothing, not even a bottle of water. That Scott should run all the way down to the river without first consulting a map seems about right.

DAY 26
THAME

Sunday, 17 May 2009 – Thame, Sagarmatha National Park, Nepal

At six o'clock I hear Ivan get up, pack his things and leave the room. By the time I pack at seven and head for breakfast he's already gone, presumably hoping to find his friend Scott in the next village, Marulung.

I get away at eight o'clock. It's a cold and misty morning again. Looking up towards the pass I see a light dusting of snow on the foothills just above the village, and realise there must be a lot more snow on the Renjo La 1,000m above, perhaps covering all our tracks from yesterday. I'm relieved I made the decision to cross the pass when I did – it may have been my one and only chance.

The first hour of the walk this morning has a back-end-of-nowhere feel to it; although herders' cottages dot the hillsides and valley, I feel entirely alone in a vast, peaceful landscape. The valley I'm walking through, the Bhote Khosi, has been a trade route between Nepal and Tibet for centuries. The famous (and sometimes infamous) Nangpa La pass marks the border at its northern end. Originally Tibetans, the Sherpas migrated into Nepal over the Nangpa La, probably in the 16th century. The name *Sherpa* means *easterner* because they originally came from the Tibetan region of Kham to the east.

They were mostly traders who made a secondary living by farming. Unlike Nepalis from the south, they were used to the high desert climate of Tibet and easily settled in the mountain region of Solu-Khumbu. The Sherpas made their home here, growing crops on the fertile slopes, and trading with their kinsmen across the Nangpa La in Tibet. Since they arrived, wheat, rice, millet and vegetables have passed north from Nepal, while salt, wool, skins and religious texts have come the other way. There have been moments since the Chinese occupation of Tibet in the 1950s when thousands of refugees have poured across the pass. Now, hearing nothing but the river crashing below me, I find this hard to imagine. The land is barren and sandy and covered in rocks, and I like to think it has a Tibetan feel to it.

After two hours of walking I have descended about 500m and reached the first patches of grassland. Huge snow-capped mountains loom somewhere high above me, but today they are hidden in cloud and only the occasional glimpse of a massive rock wall encased in ice reminds me of their presence. I round a corner and start to find myself in civilisation as the suburbs of Thame reveal themselves across a huge bend in the river. Villages, stupas, mani walls, and the occasional painted teahouse dot the area.

When I reach Thame, I don't recognise it for what it is. The village is famous for being an ancient trading centre and the birthplace of Tenzing Norgay (the first man to climb Everest along with Edmund Hillary). In fact, Tenzing himself explained in his autobiography that although his family lived in Thame and he grew up there, he was born in a place called Tsa-chu, close to Makalu.

I'm expecting a crowded, bustling village of narrow alleyways, but instead I look down from a hillside onto a flat plain of fields partitioned by stone walls. Most of the houses in the village are spread far apart on corners of field boundaries, with just a small cluster towards the top end. I descend to the plain, but then I can't find a way into the village – there appear to be no pathways. I have to climb back up to the hillside again to look for the way in and a route between fields.

From the top of the hill I make a mental note of three likely looking teahouses, and memorise the routes to reach them. When I get to my first choice I can see the front door open, but I walk all the way around it without finding a gate into the compound. I go to my second choice and walk straight into a corridor full of bedrooms, but nobody greets me and I can't find the dining room. Then, at my third choice, the Thame View Lodge, everything falls into place: there is a nice dining room, clean toilets, running water, and a proprietor who tells me he's climbed

Everest, Cho Oyu, Makalu and Manaslu (there are signed summit photos on the dining-room wall to prove it). I must have been destined to come here. Big bottles of Chinese Lhasa beer are available for 350 rupees, and I decide tonight might be the time to break my self-imposed Khumbu alcohol ban. It's perfect – and I selfishly keep my fingers crossed the Adventure Consultants group doesn't turn up later and take the place over.

Thame Monastery perching on a hill above the village

After lunch, I wander up through junipers to the monastery high above the village. The setting is fabulous, and I'm so glad I chose to stay a night here. After visiting the peaceful monastery, I keep walking a little further and a little higher, lost in thought and enjoying the moment. I have a bookmark from the

Pilgrim's Book House in Kathmandu inscribed with a quotation by W.H. Murray, the Scottish climber and mountaineering writer who travelled in Nepal in the 1950s.

The art of Himalayan travel – and indeed of all adventure – is the art of being bold enough to enjoy life now.

While I can think of more appropriate adjectives than *bold*, I wholeheartedly agree with the general sentiment. Don't think about the past, or about all the places you've been and the things you've done; don't think about the future, about where you're going next, or what you will do when you get back. If you do that then you've missed something important. Just appreciate where you are and what you are doing in the present moment – and enjoy it. As I descend along the pathway clad with juniper high above an alpine valley, with the monastery on the hill ahead of me, Thame far below, and occasional glimpses of Kangtega and Thamserku in the clouds miles above, I don't forget these words.

When I return to the village, I see the leader of the Adventure Consultants group wandering around the garden of another lodge. As I approach along the path he turns his back and ignores me, but I don't mind – I'll have my lodge all to myself.

DAY 27
NAMCHE THE BUILDING SITE

Monday, 18 May 2009 – Namche Bazaar, Sagarmatha
National Park, Nepal

It's a fine morning and the skies are clear, revealing the view of Kongde high above Thame. Kangtega and Thamserku skulked beneath clouds yesterday afternoon, but now they rise majestically down the valley. Since photographic conditions are better this morning, after breakfast I decide to go for another walk up the hill to the monastery. I'm thrilled to see a rare Impeyan pheasant – the national symbol of Nepal, with its broad blue back and distinctive crown on its forehead – appear out of the undergrowth and flutter away before me.

I leave Thame at nine o'clock and cross the river almost immediately. The trail to Namche begins as a path cut into a cliff face high above a gorge, and the river crashes far below all morning, but the valley broadens, passing through pleasant grassy banks lined with juniper.

After descending through a couple of villages crammed with mani walls, the landscape starts to feel less remote. These walls are made from stones painted with Buddhist symbols, and I soon begin to find them irritating. For reasons of religious sensitivity, I'm supposed to pass them clockwise, but the left-hand trail around their sides is often ridiculously narrow with additional steep ascent – I don't appreciate the interruption to my slow plod. I frequently ignore them and keep ahead along the main trail, my pack sitting heavy on my shoulders. There's enough up and down on this trail without making it harder for myself. While I usually follow the custom in Nepal and pass to the left of them, during this stretch of the trail there are so many that I decide I've had enough of the superstitious nonsense.

As I approach Namche, the path passes through cool pine forest with more ascent than I was prepared for. A ludicrous maze of mani-stone madness greets my arrival above Namche. A huge area of the hillside has been dug up, and it looks to be destined for some sort of mani-stone theme park. I negotiate my way through the rubble and dirt and arrive above the horseshoe-shaped bowl that contains the capital of Sherpa country.

The village has grown since I was last here. Huge lodges are squeezed together around all three hillsides; every square inch of space that isn't a lodge soon will be. The *tap tap tap* of hammer on stone echoes around the valley. Namche is one huge building site.

Thamserku rises above Namche Bazaar

I check in to the Khumbu Lodge, which is unrecognisable since I last visited – it has expanded considerably. I chuckle to myself when I see the Adventure Consultants group sitting at a table across the huge dining hall. Of all the dozens of lodges there are in Namche, that I should end up at the same one as them… again. I can't seem to shake them off, but the noodles I have for lunch are the best I've had all trip.

I decide to go outside for a walk around the village, or perhaps *town* would be a better word to describe it now. Namche enjoys a setting like nowhere else in the world, perched in a bowl 500m above the gorge of the Bhote Khosi River. The mountain Kongde Ri, with its many jagged snow-capped summits, dominates the town more than 2,000m above it on the other side of the valley. The colourful buildings form a semicircle around the bowl facing Kongde Ri. Most of the buildings here now seem to be hotels and commercial properties. Each street curls around steeply on a higher level to the preceding one, so the buildings appear to be piled on top of one another. Above the town the hillside keeps rising. Pathways fan out over it to the next big Sherpa villages of Khunde and Khumjung. I remember the setting well from when I was here seven years ago, but the village has expanded beyond all recognition – I expect it will be bigger still when I return, whenever that may be.

DAY 28
THE BUSY EVEREST TRAIL

Tuesday, 19 May 2009 – Lukla, Solu-Khumbu, Nepal

I have a long day ahead of me, so I take a 6.30 breakfast. Consulting my guidebook for walking times, I mentally divide the day into three-hour intervals. There are three of them: Namche to Monjo, Monjo to Phakding, and Phakding to Lukla. I'm away before seven o'clock and descend steeply through pine forest to the junction of the Bhote Khosi and Dudh Khosi rivers. Here a suspension bridge crosses the latter and the two rivers merge, continuing as the Dudh Khosi, which I follow for the rest of the day.

This first section is pleasantly cool in shade and nobody seems to be about, except for a handful of frail old folk tottering on their walking poles as they descend the path. I wonder why some people leave it so late in life to come and see Everest. The trail requires a decent degree of fitness and the walk up to Namche must have nearly killed them. Are our lives so busy that we can't get the time off to explore the world more while we are working, or does the dream to see the Himalayas come late for some of us?

Beyond the junction, the path passes through a wide, bouldery river bed before climbing high and continuing through pine forest. The villages resume with the settlement of Jorsale, and from here the path is an almost perpetual sprawl of Sherpa villages lined with teahouses and trekking accommodation (my favourite is one called the Beer Garden Lodge). All are smarter than they looked last time I came this way, and I meet more and more trekkers as I continue.

I reach the national park office at Monjo at 8.30, an hour and a half ahead of my estimated schedule. Here I dig out all the paperwork Siling gave me before we parted a week ago – my trekker's registration card, Makalu-Barun National Park entry permit, Mera Peak climbing permit, and Island Peak climbing permit – but nothing satisfies the man at the desk, who keeps demanding 1,000 rupees off me, without explaining why. It seems his English isn't good enough to cope with any conversation beyond asking for money. In the end I have no option but to pay.

It's only later that I realise he gave me an entry permit for Sagarmatha National Park as well; it's the only bit of paper I didn't have because we entered the park over a high pass, the Amphu Labtsa, where there were no checkpoints. It's not a huge sum of money – the equivalent of US$10 – and it's probably justified. I don't know how much I've paid in total for all my various permits, but the gruff demand this time has left a slightly sour taste in the mouth.

I continue through increasing heat, and pass through Phakding at 10.30, still well ahead of schedule. Although the valley is pleasant and green, the endless succession of villages becomes monotonous. The valley walls are steep. Only occasional glimpses of snow peaks can be seen. The searing heat saps my energy, and the ridiculous number of mani walls continues to grate. I've always been tolerant of these in the past, but every five minutes it seems there is yet another one sending me wearily off on a steep path into the undergrowth in my bid to avoid upsetting the locals by walking past anticlockwise. The theory is that the prayers inscribed upon them, *Om Mani Padme Hum* (which translates meaninglessly as 'hail to the jewel in the lotus'), are echoed by the wind as you walk past. If you circle the stones the wrong way it therefore causes the words to be uttered backwards. Personally, I can live with this, even if backwards it spells a rude word, but according to custom I don't accumulate as much merit as I do when I walk around the correct way.

Believing this concept to be preposterous, I pointedly start ignoring all rules and walk past them any way I choose. Occasionally, when no one is looking, I make a 'V' sign at them. Perhaps the gods are watching; perhaps they're not. The main thing is that it gives me a measure of satisfaction.

The approach to Lukla is a steep climb up steps; I'm sweating like a pig by the time I get there. I crash out on a bench in the North Face Lodge shortly before one o'clock, having completed the walk from Namche in around six hours with barely a break. I check the altimeter on my watch and discover that I've ascended and descended 16,160m in the last month. That's the height of two 8,000m peaks from sea level. I've earned a rest. I cheer up my stomach by ordering Sprite, hot lemon, and fried noodles in quick succession, but the episode with the trekking permit lingers at the back of my mind. These little setbacks often seem to come in threes. What else am I going to have problems with – my flight, or my hotel room in Kathmandu?

These thoughts are forgotten when I retreat to my room at the North Face. The room is spacious, with two low beds in what I imagine to be Japanese style. The sun flickers through a partially drawn curtain and the room is pleasantly warm. It's also en suite, with my own wash basin and western-style sit-down toilet in an attached bathroom. Although basic by western standards, with no other furniture, this is the most comfortable accommodation I've enjoyed for a month.

Now that I have a chance to relax, I realise that a combination of the searing heat, national park permit, inexplicable number of mani walls, and relentless plodding up and down hills with a heavy pack has made me bad tempered. This is foolish. I'm in an amazing location and have had a wonderful month exploring it. My boots have even lasted the whole trek without falling apart, something I never imagined possible when I first discovered the damage in Tangnag. With my walking over and this thought in my mind, I crash out on one of the beds and sleep soundly for two hours.

The lodge is quiet this evening. I'm half-expecting the Adventure Consultants group to walk through the door, but for once I'm deprived of their company. There are only four other people staying here besides myself. I sit in a quiet dining room reading my book and enjoying a couple of cans of Tuborg beer. A member of staff from the lodge has been down to the Yeti Airlines office on my behalf, and tells me I don't have to be at the airport until eight o'clock tomorrow, so I can have a leisurely wake-up. I book a seven o'clock breakfast.

DAY 29
LUKLA TO KATHMANDU

Wednesday, 20 May 2009 – Kathmandu, Nepal

I'm in the middle of a six o'clock bowel movement when I hear banging on my door. I engage in a conversation through the wall as I sit on the toilet. There's been a change of plan, I'm told. I'm now due to be on the first flight out of Lukla, and I'm supposed to be at the airport at six o'clock.

'But it's six o'clock now,' I say.

'Yes, sir. Come quickly, breakfast ready.'

Kit is strewn across the room. I stuff away my sleeping bag and down jacket and cram everything inside my rucksack as quickly as I can. Fortunately, I've been doing this for a few days now and I know how everything fits together. Even so, it's 6.20 by the time I'm ready, and I don't know whether I'll have time for breakfast. Fried eggs, toast and tea appear on a table in front of me as soon as I go upstairs to the dining room. I overhear a conversation on the next table stating that the first flight is at seven o'clock. In ten very brisk minutes I stuff my face and pay my bill.

'You have my ticket?' I ask the man who woke me up.

'Nick has it,' he replies. 'He's at the airport. You're a lucky man.'

Nick, I think to myself? Since when has there ever been a Sherpa called Nick?

I speed-walk through the village and arrive at the airport in just five minutes. 'Nick', who arranged my flight yesterday, is waiting at the check-in area and has been looking out for me. He is indeed a Sherpa, though I suspect that Nick is not his real name.

'You're a lucky man,' he says as he greets me.

He checks in my bag himself and asks for 170 rupees for the airport tax. He vanishes and reappears a moment later with a tax receipt and my boarding card. It's all incredibly efficient, and I barely have time to thank him before I'm ushered through security. By 6.45 I'm waiting comfortably in the tiny departure lounge with maybe fifty to a hundred other tourists, all of whom believe themselves to be on the first flight. To think that only forty-five minutes earlier I was still completing my morning business.

Within minutes, half a dozen tiny Twin Otter planes have landed in quick succession on the airstrip, unloaded their passengers, and turned back to Kathmandu for their return flights. Mine is the sixth and last of them. By 7.20 I have squeezed myself onto the plane, and I feel it drop down the short, steep runway and off the end into the Dudh Khosi Valley. Moments later it rises again and begins to lift over the mountains.

Our tiny plane passes through thick cloud and it suddenly becomes very dark. This is perhaps the first time I've ever been on a flight when I can feel the aircraft getting battered by the rain. We feel ourselves judder from side to side, but everyone remains calm. The staff at the lodge were right about my being lucky. The conditions are atrocious and I can't imagine there will be another flight out of Lukla after this one. The clouds are high above Kathmandu Airport; it's a big relief when we drop beneath them and touch down safely.

By 9.30 I'm checking in to the Hotel Shanker. I've arrived a day or two sooner than they were expecting, but it's late in the season and there's a room available.

'You are lucky,' the lady on reception says to me.

I am. Up in my room, I take a shower and wash all the accumulated dirt of a month away. I have a shave to get rid of a month's growth. I contemplate the three days in Kathmandu ahead of me. I see myself spending much of the time sitting in garden bars, drinking Everest beer. Perhaps I'll do some sightseeing. Who knows.

But one thing I do know. This morning, they have all been right.

I'm a lucky man.

ACKNOWLEDGEMENTS

Thanks to Mark Dickson for being entertaining company on this and many other expeditions to the Himalayas over the years.

We were indebted to our kitchen crew: Sarki the cook, Pasang the assistant cook, and kitchen assistants Gombu and Karma. And to our eight porters from the Makalu region, who were some of the best, most reliable and cheerful porters I have ever trekked with: Bujung, Drukchen, Lhakpa, Pema, Pemba, Tashi, Temba and Wongchu.

Thanks to Dawa Bhote for being a safe and reliable climbing guide. Most of all, thanks are due to Siling Ghale for his logistical expertise, patience and humility. Even for some of his jokes. An extra nod of thanks to Tina Stacey for her assistance with trip planning.

Thanks to Ade Summers for accompanying us much of the way as he led a group for KE Adventure Travel.

I should also express my gratitude to the many solo and independent trekkers who made cameo appearances in this book as a result of my bumping into them in teahouses during my foray into the Gokyo Valley.

Thanks to my editor, Alex Roddie, for his help polishing the text.

Most of all thanks to all of you, readers of my blog and diaries. I hope you have enjoyed this one, and I look forward to welcoming you back sometime. If you have not read it already then I hope you will enjoy my first full-length book, *Seven Steps from Snowdon to Everest*, about my ten-year journey from hill walker to Everest climber.

SEVEN STEPS FROM SNOWDON TO EVEREST

A hill walker's journey to the top of the world

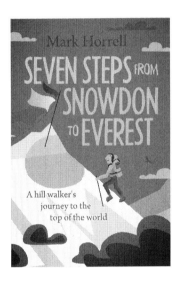

As he teetered on a narrow rock ledge a yak's bellow short of the stratosphere, with a rubber mask strapped to his face, a pair of mittens the size of a sealion's flippers, and a drop of two kilometres below him, it's fair to say Mark Horrell wasn't entirely happy with the situation he found himself in.

He was an ordinary hiker who had only read books about mountaineering, and little did he know when he signed up for an organised trek in Nepal with a group of elderly ladies that ten years later he would be attempting to climb the world's highest mountain.

But as he travelled across the Himalayas, Andes, Alps and East Africa, following in the footsteps of the pioneers, he dreamed up a seven-point plan to gain the skills and experience which could turn a wild idea into reality.

Funny, incisive and heartfelt, his journey provides a refreshingly honest portrait of the joys and torments of a modern-day Everest climber.

First published in 2015. A list of bookstores can be found on Mark's website:

www.markhorrell.com/SnowdonToEverest

PHOTOGRAPHS

I hope you enjoyed the photos in this book. Thanks to the miracles of the internet you can view all the photos from my Solu-Khumbu trek online via the photo-sharing website *Flickr*.

Mera, Island & the Gokyo Lakes. Nepal, April/May, 2009:

www.markhorrell.com/MeraIsland

ABOUT THE AUTHOR

Since 2010 Mark Horrell has written what has been described as one of the most credible Everest opinion blogs out there. He writes about trekking and mountaineering from the often silent perspective of the commercial client.

For over a decade he has been exploring the world's greater mountain ranges and keeping a diary of his travels. As a writer he strives to do for mountain history what Bill Bryson did for long-distance hiking.

Several of his expedition diaries are available as quick reads from the major online bookstores. His first full-length book, *Seven Steps from Snowdon to Everest*, about his ten-year journey from hill walker to Everest climber, was published in November 2015.

His favourite mountaineering book is *The Ascent of Rum Doodle* by W.E. Bowman.

ABOUT THIS SERIES

The *Footsteps on the Mountain Travel Diaries* are Mark's expedition journals. Quick reads, they are lightly edited versions of what he scribbles in his tent each evening after a day in the mountains.

For other titles in this series see Mark's website: www.markhorrell.com/diaries

CONNECT

You can join Mark's **mailing list** to keep updated:
www.markhorrell.com/mailinglist

Website and blog: www.markhorrell.com
Twitter: @markhorrell
Facebook:
www.facebook.com/footstepsonthemountain
Flickr: www.flickr.com/markhorrell
YouTube: www.youtube.com/markhorrell

DID YOU ENJOY THIS BOOK?

Thank you for buying and reading this book. Word-of-mouth is crucial for any author to be successful. If you enjoyed it then please consider leaving a review. Even if it's only a couple of sentences, it would be a great help and will be appreciated enormously.

Links to this book on the main online book stores can be found on Mark's website:
www.markhorrell.com/IslandsInTheSnow

33021527R00099

Printed in Poland
by Amazon Fulfillment
Poland Sp. z o.o., Wrocław